By Mercy's Light

*Daily Reflections on Divine Mercy
from Ash Wednesday to Divine Mercy Sunday*

Fr. Michael T. Mitchell

To Faustina, in return for much

TABLE OF CONTENTS

INTRODUCTION

I first became familiar with the spirituality of Divine Mercy long before I started the actual writing of this book. I was a seminarian in Rome at the time, and my understanding of Divine Mercy was cursory at best. I still remember that day in March 2009, when a copy of St. Faustina's *Diary* inexplicably appeared outside the door of my room. It was an English copy, something rare in my Italian seminary. I have no idea who put it there, but that book came into my life at a moment when I deeply needed to hear its message. I credit the message of Divine Mercy for helping me through those last years of seminary. It has powerfully impacted my personal life and ministry, and I will forever be indebted to St. Faustina and her mysterious "apostle of Divine Mercy" for leaving me her diary.

For those who are unfamiliar with Divine Mercy, this book will be a good starting place. Faustina was a pious nun from Poland. She was blessed with receiving many divine messages via private revelations in the 1930s. She wrote them down at the request of her superiors and spiritual directors. Those writings are what we know today as the *Diary of Saint Maria Faustina Kowalska*.

The diary that Faustina kept is much more than the retelling of the personal life and thoughts of a pious nun in Poland. It was by means of her diary that Jesus chose to reveal his message of Divine Mercy to the whole Church. Jesus often dictated to her what she should write, and that is why Jesus called her his "secretary of mercy." Page after page of spiritual gems can be mined from its depths. Sections on the Eucharist, prayer, confession, the nature of the Church, the love of God for each soul, purgatory, and heaven keep me coming back for more and take me deeper each time. It is this treasure trove that I hope to introduce you to through my poor words. Even now, as I come to the end of this work, I feel I have barely scratched the surface.

I encourage you to read Faustina's *Diary* in your own time, slowly and prayerfully. It is rich and speaks eloquently on its own. This book you hold in your hands is not an exposition of the *Diary*, but rather the fruit of my own years of prayerful reflection. I have deliberately opted to avoid stringing together quote after quote from the *Diary* in a way that simply repeats the message. I hope—and in fact intend—that you, the reader, would read this book with the *Diary* of Faustina close at hand. I have included all the references to the *Diary* as footnotes for easy study.

This book is one of spiritual theology, not dogma; it's a work dedicated to helping Christians grow in their holiness and devotion. As spiritual theology, this book focuses on the experiential dimension of our Catholic faith, how mysteries such as God's divine mercy may be received within the context of Christian living. For these reasons, it is important to remember as you read this book that I have permitted myself a certain literary license in creating the reflections in this book. There are many details that Faustina never mentions in her writings, and as with Scripture itself, it is possible to sometimes "read between the lines" or make some educated guesswork. Thus, the reflections in this book are mine and do not represent any official statement on Divine Mercy. For those, you will need visit the Marian Fathers at the National Shrine of Divine Mercy or visit their webpages.[1]

How to Use This Book

The book is designed to be a daily Lenten devotional. For each day of Lent—from Ash Wednesday and into the Easter season finishing

---

1 I suggest these three: www.thedivinemercy.org, www.marian.org, and www.shrineofdivinemercy.org.

on Divine Mercy Sunday—I have provided a spiritual reflection about Divine Mercy. The reflections loosely will follow themes of preparation for Divine Mercy, the revelations of Divine Mercy themselves, living out Divine Mercy in our lives, and ending with reflections on a Church of Mercy.

The reflections will include a few passages that you may read from the *Diary*. These should be read prior to reading the reflection. *By Mercy's Light* and Faustina's *Diary* will be your guides throughout the Lenten journey.

If you would like to use this book outside of Lent, that will be easy enough. The reflections have Lenten themes but are not limited in scope by this. Anytime of the year would be fine. I would encourage starting on a Wednesday, so the days will match up easier.

In group settings, I would invite the group to read aloud together the numbers from the *Diary* and have a moment of personal sharing as to the meaning of the *Diary* for today.

For any error that may be in these pages, I ask your pardon. For any profit you might gain from my words, I give thanks and place them before the throne of the Giver of all gifts. Finally, I thank you for embracing this book. My prayers go with you as you embark on this with *By Mercy's Light*. I pray that however this book came to be in your possession, St. Faustina walks with you and intercedes for you just as she has done for me!

Fr. Michael Mitchell
November, 2021
Feast of All Saints

ASH WEDNESDAY

KEEPING CHRIST IN OUR LENTEN JOURNEY

Just as, in a physical body, the head and members all aid one another, so too, between Christ and ourselves, there is a mutual exchange of good things: we share in His inheritance, functions and dignities, in His Kingdom, priesthood, etc. It is a source of true joy that Christ is to us a Brother, a real Man; that we can go to Him without any fear; that we can love Him, even though we may be sunk in the deepest misery and all the degradation of sin. This trust in His Mercy is the most wonderful result of the Incarnation and, as it were, the final expression of the Prophet's hymn: "Behold, God is my Savior, I will deal confidently, and will not fear" (Isaiah 12:2).
BLESSED MICHAEL SOPOCKO, 46[2]

Readings from the **Diary:** *618, 1273, 1625*

Today, you begin the season of Lent under the protection of Divine Mercy. You will go hand in hand with St. Faustina, at times with Blessed Michael Sopocko, and always under the merciful gaze of Christ. Lent prepares us to accompany Our Lord in his passion, and Holy Week ushers us into the greatest of Christian mysteries. The climax of Divine Mercy is going to be experienced at the foot of the Cross when Jesus says the words "Father, into your hands I commend my spirit!" (Luke 23:46).

---

2 Quotes from Blessed Michael Sopocko, unless otherwise noted, are taken from his book *The Mercy of God in His Works* (Stockbridge, MA: Marian Fathers, 1962).

This offering of Our Lord to his Father is at one and the same time both the moment of destroying death and sin and also the tender moment of union between Jesus and the Father. Jesus lays down his life by placing himself in the arms of his Father. This is a tender image of God the Father, who was not far away from Jesus in the moment of his passion. Rather, the Father was very near his Son on the cross as he received his Son's sacrifice. Today, this tenderness of God the Father is also available to us, for Divine Mercy is God's tender love meeting us in our weakness of sin.

To live a Lent with Divine Mercy means to live Lent near to the heart of God the Father. It means to personally touch Christ this Lent. It is to allow the Father to embrace you, to save you and lift you up. Despite its simplicity, this is no easy task. For some reason our hearts and souls can strongly resist this embrace of mercy.

The season of Lent has a penitential aspect to it. The Church today invites us to begin a season of fasting, prayer, and almsgiving. It is important to understand the deepest truth in these three realities as we set out on this journey.

First, in fasting, a Christian may lessen the amount of food eaten, may forsake certain types of food, or may go without food altogether for a time. The amount and style of fasting is personal. But what is common to all Christians is that we refrain from food in some fashion *in order to await the coming of the wedding feast of the Lamb*. We will one day eat and drink in the Kingdom of Heaven. To fast is to remember the very words of Jesus at the end of the Last Supper: "I tell you, I will never again drink of this fruit of the vine until that day when I drink it new with you in my Father's kingdom" (Matthew 26:29).

To await with joy and longing for the beginning of the heavenly feast is to remember this biblical truth. We fast because we want to be with Christ the Bridegroom. We fast because we want to wait for him to come to the home of our hearts before we begin the feast. Without Christ there simply *is* no feast. Only with Christ can we joyfully celebrate. This is why fasting is a prophetic sign; it points to a future heavenly reality.

We normally wait to begin a meal with family and friends. Only once all have arrived at the feast do we begin. What we do for one another we also can do for God. The Christian sense of fasting is preparing ourselves for the arrival of the Bridegroom. As Jesus says, "The wedding guests cannot mourn as long as the bridegroom is with them, can they? The days will come when the bridegroom is taken away from them, and then they will fast" (Matthew 9:15).

Today, if we fast, it is because we are thinking of the Bridegroom first and foremost. We are not merely refraining from food for the sake of personal discipline, as if somehow our suffering here on earth were pleasing to the Father. No good father wants to see his children hungry.

Secondly, the almsgiving of a Christian has a deeply Christological nature. When the Church invites us to give alms, it is not because the Church has a goal of transforming the earthly world into some utopian vision. This is not the goal or purpose of the Church. Christian charity toward one's neighbor is a consequence of Christianity, not the essence of Christianity. The essence is a person: Christ Jesus. We give alms because Jesus said, "Truly I tell you, just as you did it to one of the least of these who are members of my family, you did it to me" (Matthew 25:40). We are to give to the poor because Christ has chosen to associate himself with them on a mystical level. What drives the desire found among the saints to be with the poor is a drive to encounter Christ.

Material goods distract us from those goods that are spiritual. Making ourselves excessively comfortable here on earth causes us to forget the spiritual goods of the life to come. Material well-being can easily become all consuming. We even begin to project this on to God, assuming that God's will is for all of us to be well fed, to receive medicines, to go to good schools and colleges, to own houses and cars, and to be happy. This rather non-Gospel-centered vision is one that needs to be purified. God's will is that we go to heaven. Jesus never promised us that he was going to make our lives on earth easy. And so, to keep this in mind and to purify our hearts, we give away the coins of our alms as did the poor widow in the Gospel. *We do this because we know in our hearts that we need something so much more than those little coins.* We give them away without fear or concern for the future because we know we need God more than anything else. We give them away and make our future somewhat uncertain because any future without God is no future at all. And thus, we are confidently making sure that we seek God above all else.

In this, almsgiving—like fasting—is also a prophetic sign, because it points to a future that God will provide for and a future that is God's, period. Therefore, in our alms giving, we ought to see the face of Divine Mercy and, like mercy itself, stoop down to the littlest among us in order to touch that misery.

And finally, we pray. In the diary of St. Faustina, there is an emphasis on Lenten observance as a time to accompany Christ in his passion. Our Lord was very clear to Faustina throughout her life with him that his desire was to be accompanied in his passion. This is the foundation of the Catholic understanding of *consoling the Heart of Christ.* Today Jesus invites you deeper into the Garden of Gethsemane with him. You are a chosen disciple. Let us make ready our hearts, steel our resolve, and open our souls to whichever path Our Lord choses to lead us.

THURSDAY AFTER ASH WEDNESDAY

SHARING IN THE SUFFERING
OF CHRIST WITH FAUSTINA

*Because the Lord your God is a merciful God, he will
neither abandon you nor destroy you; he will not forget the
covenant with your ancestors that he swore to them.*
DEUTERONOMY 4:31

Readings from the Diary: *618, 640, 1181, 1182*

This Lenten season, we will get to know Faustina better. Often the
lives of the saints can seem very distant from our own. We place the
saints on high pedestals, and because of this, they lose some of their
own humanity. In the end, though, when we get to know the saints,
we will find that they are more like us than we imagined. To get to
know Faustina, we have to look at perhaps one of the most important
characteristics of all the saints: they lived for Christ.

To know and understand Faustina, we must remember the One
who was the center of her life: Our Lord Jesus Christ. There is a passage
from her *Diary* that gives a glimpse into her soul.

It happened on a Thursday evening. Once Faustina joined her
religious congregation, she had the custom of making an extra hour
of prayer every Thursday. In this hour, the theme of the prayer was
to remember the hours spent by Jesus in the Garden of Olives, and

especially his request that we spend an hour with him (see Matthew 26:40). On this particular Thursday, Faustina's convent was celebrating the Christmas season. This Christmas festivities brought a change of schedule to the routine of convent life. With the festivities interrupting her normal schedule, Faustina lost track of the days and completely forgot that it was Thursday. Without realizing it, the day passed by, and Faustina did not make her extra hour of prayer. When she lay down for the night she could not fall asleep. She began to think about the day and felt that she was forgetting something. Jesus then appeared at her bedside. He was suffering immensely in his mystical passion. He said:

> *I have been waiting to share My suffering with you,*
> *for who can understand My suffering better than My*
> *spouse?* (*Diary*, 348)

Jesus is asking Faustina to console him in this manner of mystical prayer. Somehow, Faustina was able to comfort Our Lord from her own historical moment in time. This facet of prayer is often forgotten. This Lenten season, Our Lord is coming to you to make the same request. Will you spend this lent with him?

When we go to prayer, we come away changed. While at times imperceptible, we certainly are different after we come away from a moment of time with God. But what about for God? Does God change because of our prayer? On the one hand, God is unchanging by his very essence. But yet, through Christ the Son we have a doorway into the heart of God. Through Christ, in a mystical way, our prayer changes God. Jesus is not indifferent to our free choice to partake of his chalice. Faustina learned this well. You will be keeping our Lord company as you make this Lenten journey!

FRIDAY AFTER ASH WEDNESDAY

JESUS, A MAN WHO CALLS

Mercy is a particular mode of love, such that when love encounters suffering,
it takes action to do something about it. It is making someone else's
pain our own. Mercy is love in action.
FR. DONALD CALLOWAY, MIC[3]

Readings from the **Diary***: 1008, 1017, 1275*

Throughout the Gospels, Jesus calls people to follow him. The first action of his public ministry is to seek out and name the Twelve Apostles. He wastes no time and seems to have mapped out his first journey through the Holy Land specifically to encounter each one. This penchant of Jesus, to call apostles to himself and transform them into laborers in his vineyard, continues to this day.

The call of Christ is a gift of Divine Mercy no matter when it comes, and Christians of all walks of life are called. The idea of a "vocation" is often linked primarily to a priest or religious sister. But there is a broader meaning of the word. The word vocation comes from Latin, meaning "to call." All people are called to holiness. "All the faithful, whatever their condition or state . . . are called by the Lord to that perfection of sanctity by which the Father himself is perfect."[4]

---

3 Fr. Donald Calloway, *Beautiful Mercy* (North Palm Beach, FL: Wellspring, 2015).
4 *Lumen Gentium*, 11. Also see *CCC*, 825.

Grace always takes the first step toward us. The presence of God in the world is a hidden one, yet the effects of his presence can be clearly seen. The Christian life is ultimately vocational. It begins with a call that is repeated over and over throughout one's life. So, these vocations, these "calls of Jesus," are gifts of mercy to the Church. A person who receives the invitation to follow Jesus more closely receives not just a personal gift, but a gift for the whole Church.

At seven years of age, Faustina heard this call of God for the first time. It marked the beginning of a lifelong love affair between her soul and the very heart of God. The call came to Faustina in Poland in 1912. To put it into perspective, it was the year the *Titanic* had set sail. Ronald Reagan was a one-year-old boy just learning to walk. World War I was about to start. As is often the case with the works of God, unnoticed to the world, a young girl named Helena lived on a farm in Glogowiec, which lies in the heart of modern-day Poland. She was the future Saint Faustina, Apostle of Divine Mercy.

Baptized as Helena Kowalska, her future religious name, and the name she will forever be remembered by, was Maria Faustina of the Most Blessed Sacrament. She was the third of ten living children. As one of the oldest, she helped raise her siblings while working on the family farm. A chance at higher education was never within her grasp, and a life of hard work and eventually a family of her own was her only real future.

Faustina herself begins her story at the age of seven. She writes in her journal that even at that young age, she felt God speak to her soul and offer her "an invitation to a more perfect life."

She does not tell us where and how this took place but only that it was a voice from God. It is remarkable that at such a young age, she knew she was destined to be a religious sister. This would not be the first time a saint of the Church was called as a child. A vocation is a call from God that can and does come at any age and any time. However, while Faustina knew God was calling her to be a religious sister, she did not know how, when, or where this was to happen.

SATURDAY AFTER ASH WEDNESDAY

THE RICH YOUNG MAN

When those who follow Jesus seek out the afflicted and comfort them in their misery, they are revealing the very heart of God, who is rich in mercy (see Eph 2:4). To take notice of needs and afflictions is the first step of mercy. To step out of my own needs and my own preoccupation and take notice, and then to move into another's life with comfort, is not only a revelation of the nature of the universe and the God who freely chose to create it, it is also the key to unlocking God's mercy in our own lives.

CURTIS MARTIN[5]

Readings from the **Diary:** *713, 1681, 1682*

A deep yearning for God exists in every human heart, but often it is drowned out because of the noise and distractions of life. The Gospel tells us of an encounter between Jesus and a young man who keenly felt this tension (see Mark 10:17–31). This young man had in his heart a sincere desire to be righteous before God. This yearning for more is what prompted him, someone who had everything he could want materially, to seek out Jesus. His question, "What do I still lack?" reveals that amid all this material wealth there was still a spiritual emptiness in his heart.

Mark's Gospel says that Jesus "looked at him and loved him," then called him. The Heart of Mercy himself looked beyond appearances

---

5 Curtis Martin, *Beautiful Mercy* (North Palm Beach, FL: Wellspring, 2015), 101.

into the soul of this man and saw a life of many offerings to God, but never a complete holocaust of self. Jesus challenged this young man to make a lifestyle out of his generosity, to give his whole life to God, and not just a portion of his wealth.

This challenge was—and is—a hard one. It is not at its root about material possessions. All of us are challenged to a wholehearted self-giving to God of trust and abandonment. There is no easy way around this, yet the reward in store for a simple "yes" is unbelievable. Our yes is not a command of Jesus, however. He says to the young man, "If you wish to be perfect" (Matthew 19:21). Jesus respects our freedom. He does not command, but rather invites.

A "yes" to Divine Mercy in your own life is to open a door through which Christ can bring his infinite mercy to others. It is stepping out into the life of mercy that changes the world. Faustina's "yes" was an important part of the history of the twentieth century. St. John Paul II canonized St. Faustina in April 2000. He said in his homily:

> *Today my joy is truly great in presenting the life and witness of Sr. Faustina Kowalska to the whole Church as a gift of God for our time. By divine Providence, the life of this humble daughter of Poland was completely linked with the history of the 20th century, the century we have just left behind. In fact, it was between the First and Second World Wars that Christ entrusted his message of mercy to her. Those who remember, who were witnesses and participants in the events of those years and the horrible sufferings they caused for millions of people, know well how necessary was the message of mercy.*
>
> *Jesus told Sr Faustina: "Humanity will not find peace until it turns trustfully to divine mercy" (Diary, p. 132). Through the work of the Polish religious, this message*

has become linked for ever to the 20th century, the last of the second millennium and the bridge to the third. It is not a new message but can be considered a gift of special enlightenment that helps us to relive the Gospel of Easter more intensely, to offer it as a ray of light to the men and women of our time.[6]

FIRST SUNDAY OF LENT

VOCATION AS INVITATION

*Throughout the centuries many men and women, transformed by divine
love, have consecrated their lives to the cause of the Kingdom. Already on
the shores of the Sea of Galilee, many allowed themselves to be won by Jesus:
they were in search of healing in body or spirit, and they were touched by
the power of his grace. Others were chosen personally by Him and became
his apostles. We also find some, like Mary Magdalene and others, who
followed him on their own initiative, simply out of love. Like the disciple
John, they too found a special place in his heart. These men and women,
who knew the mystery of the love of the Father through Jesus, represent the
variety of vocations which have always been present in the Church.*

POPE BENEDICT XVI[7]

Readings from the **Diary***: 6, 7, 8*

When Faustina first heard the call to follow Jesus, she received it as
it truly was: an invitation. If we divorce the "invitation" from the
call, we risk misunderstanding what a vocation is altogether. In her
diary, Faustina directly refers to her vocation as an "invitation to a
more perfect life" (*Diary*, 7). This core word invitation, is one of the
foundations of a vocation.

---

7 Pope Benedict XVI, Message for the 43rd World Day of Prayer for Vocations, May 2006.

A vocation is not something imposed by God upon a person's life. It is not a destiny that we must follow or risk forever living outside God's will. That said, God does have a beautiful plan in mind for each and every person and following this divine plan is a way to encounter the joy and peace of a life lived with God. The process of discovering and adhering to this plan has led many souls down the path of sanctity and mission. And in each and every case, human freedom is respected. *Ultimately, God's plan is that we respond to his call in love.* Our free response of love is his will for us.

Faustina's free will is evident by her own admission of not living according "to the call of grace" (*Diary*, 8). She had many cares to worry about at home, and the hard farm life did not allow her to simply run off and join a convent.

In 1924, when Faustina was eighteen, she tried in vain to get her parents' blessing to enter a convent. It was not an easy time in Poland for Faustina's large family. Farming gave them a meager existence, and all hands were needed. In addition, admission to a convent of any type was very strict. Most convents of the time required potential candidates to provide a dowry in order to join. The ravages of the previous world war also meant that some young women were tempted to seek entrance to a convent for reasons of material security, not necessarily because of an invitation from Jesus to a religious life. To sort one group from the other, the convents made the entry process selective. Faustina, being poor and mostly uneducated, was at the bottom of the list and an unwelcome candidate. Her family could not afford to send her to a convent, and even though they were devout Catholics, her parents could not bring themselves to part from their daughter.

In the face of these difficulties and her parents' refusal, Faustina gave up trying to enter a convent, at least for a time. She admits to throwing herself into the vain things of the world. However, her heart was heavy and unsatisfied. Faustina's heart would be restless until it rested in God.

This tension between God's invitation and the pull of the world is one that many Christians have experienced. It can be a very scary position to be in. On the one hand, God's call is clear. On the other, the obstacles in pursuing his will can seem insurmountable. This crisis can lead to a person attempting to drown out the voice of God through distractions and the daily problems and amusements life provides. Thankfully, Our Lord is a merciful Savior, and he never tires of knocking on the door of our hearts.

MONDAY OF THE FIRST WEEK OF LENT

THE DANCE WITH MERCY BEGINS

"I do not pray for these only, but also for those who believe in
me through their word, that they may all be one; even as thou,
Father, art in me, and I in thee, that they also may be in us,
so that the world may believe that thou hast sent me."

JOHN 17:20–21

Readings from the **Diary***: 9, 10, 1685*

In June 1924, a town festival was held in Łódź's Venice Park. Faustina and her two sisters, like the rest of the town, were in attendance. In the evening, music and dancing began. Her *Diary* (8) seems to indicate that she was still trying to stifle the call of grace in her soul by focusing on the worldly distractions. This may have been in part her attitude as she stepped onto the dance floor at the festival. According to Ewa Czaczkowska,[8] at some point she reluctantly accepted the invitation of a young man to dance. But even so, she narrates that her soul was experiencing deep anguish. It is this moment that would change her life forever.

As Faustina began to dance, she suddenly found herself face-to-face with Jesus himself. He appeared to be in his Sacred Passion, covered in wounds and racked with pain. Jesus looked at her and said:

---

8 Ewa K. Czaczkowska, *Faustina: The Mystic and Her Message* (Stockbridge, MA: Marian Press, 2014), 59.

How long shall I put up with you and how long will you
keep putting Me off? (Diary, 9)

Faustina relates that for her the music stopped and the festival and dancing faded away. Only Jesus and Faustina remained. She doesn't relate how long this encounter lasted, only that after a time she withdrew from the dance and had to sit down. When her sister asked her why she wasn't dancing, Faustina feigned a headache. Alone and separated from the festivities, Faustina made her choice to answer Jesus who was inviting her to be with him.

This divine dance of Faustina's has a deeper meaning rooted in the theology of the Church. In Greek, the word to describe the Holy Trinity is *Perichoresis*, meaning a continual rotation, a flowing around, and a mutual indwelling and movement. Each of the Three Divine Persons centers himself upon the other two in a continual giving existence. What does the Trinity do? Theology answers with an image: They dance in a continual interchange of persons within the Divine Nature. The Godhead, even as understood from early Church times, has been explained by a dance. The call of Faustina to a more perfect life was a call for her to participate in this Divine Dance, to become a part of the Trinitarian life. This is the call of every Christian.

In a deeper way for Faustina, she was also beginning to walk toward religious vocation. For women religious, be they cloistered nuns or active sisters, their spiritual call is to accept the invitation of Christ to become his bride. They are mystically married to him alone and often wear a wedding ring to symbolize the exclusivity of their love for Jesus. In the context of Faustina's story, Jesus invites Faustina to a life of total consecration to him. He makes his move precisely when Faustina is invited to dance with another man. Jesus, who is a jealous lover, interrupts this earthly invitation with his heavenly one. Desiring her company, Jesus extends his hand to Faustina, inviting her to "dance" with him for her whole life.

This passionate side of Jesus, his impatience for souls to respond to his love, may seem like a foreign concept to some. Any study of the lives of the saints and of mystical theology, however, reveals the fiery depths of Jesus' love. As St. John of the Cross wrote, "If anyone is seeking God, the Beloved is seeking that person much more."[9]

The soul of Faustina is precious in the eyes of Christ and her vocational invitation is a fruit of this love. This moment in the life of Faustina is a grace which revealed to her a holy jealousy in the heart of Jesus for Faustina to be his own. Faustina accepted this invitation from Christ with no more hesitation and thus began the dance of her religious life.

9 St. John of the Cross, *Living Flame of Love*, 3:28.

TUESDAY OF THE FIRST WEEK OF LENT

A PATH TAKEN ONE STEP AT A TIME

At the root of every vocational journey there is the Emmanuel, the God-with-us. He shows us that we are not alone in fashioning our lives, because God walks with us, in the midst of our ups-and-downs, and, if we want him to, he weaves with each of us a marvellous tale of love, unique and irreproducible, and, at the same time, in harmony with all humanity and the entire cosmos. To discover the presence of God in our individual stories, not to feel orphans any longer, but rather to know that we have a Father in whom we can trust completely - this is the great turning-point that transforms our merely human outlook and leads man to understand, as Gaudium et spes *affirms, that he "cannot fully find himself except through a sincere gift of himself" (24).*

St. John Paul II[10]

Readings from the Diary: 10, 1692, 1693

After surrendering herself to the invitation before her, Faustina was not sure of what would come next. All she knew was that she needed to leave the dance floor of the world, to leave behind the charming music and the handsome men and dance with Jesus only. But who to tell, where to go, what convent to enter? This way of Jesus, to reveal only the incremental steps rather than the whole journey, is widely experienced by the saints throughout the centuries. It has become a principle of the

10 St. John Paul II, Message for World Day of Prayer for Vocations, May 2001.

spiritual life that often Jesus reveals only enough of his loving will to a person for them to take the next step.

We can't undervalue the sacrifice that this "next step" entails. For Faustina, the dance and the music and the people were good and beautiful things, yet unnecessary for a heart on fire for God. She was responding to a call to leave her life behind and enter into God's service as a religious sister. For this, she would only need God. All else would take second place. She began to leave the world behind, as Jesus said:

> *For he that will save his life, shall lose it: and he that shall*
> *lose his life for my sake, shall find it. (Matthew 16:25)*

This losing oneself is a painful reality. How can a soul who has encountered God's call to a religious vocation explain to a friend or family member why they are leaving behind their old life to follow Christ? Endless possibilities exist before a young woman or young man as they enter a convent or seminary, and to leave this behind is often seen as a waste of a life. But to the one called, the invitation of Christ is enough and more. It is strength for the trials ahead. In marriage it is similar. A man or woman is choosing one path by taking on their wedding vows, and they are forsaking all others. Yet a full life is one that has made real choices and decisions. Those who hesitate, who can never bring themselves to choose a path, in the end don't live any life.

Faustina left the dance that day and shut the door behind her. Part of her wanted to stay and keep a modicum of security, but Jesus had been clear. He wanted her heart, and once she answered him, there would be no turning back. From then on Faustina walked by faith alone. Nothing was clear but the next step—and even that seemed an insurmountable task.

Without knowing exactly what to do, Faustina felt drawn to the cathedral. She left the dance and her sister and friends unnoticed. Meanwhile the world and its music played on. Often the most beautiful events in this world, such as the love story between Jesus and our hearts, are a hidden secret. Media and pop culture don't remember that night as anything significant, but the story of Faustina and Jesus was just beginning.

Faustina entered the cathedral that night to lay her problems and uncertainties before Jesus. She mentions in her diary that there were a few people present, but regardless of them, she went to the front and prostrated herself in prayer. She begged God to show her the way she should walk. Her family and friends would not support her decision, and she had no money and no education with which to be accepted into a convent. Jesus was calling her, but where?

And in the stillness and prayerful environment of the cathedral, Faustina heard a voice in her soul telling her to go to Warsaw and enter a convent there (*Diary*, 10). Jesus only revealed the next step, but it was enough.

WEDNESDAY OF THE FIRST WEEK OF LENT

THE POVERTY OF CHRIST MUST BE SHARED

And he said to them: Take nothing for your journey; neither staff, nor scrip,
nor bread, nor money; neither have two coats.

LUKE 9:3

Readings from the Diary: *11, 532, 731–734*

In Luke 9:3, we hear Jesus' instructions to the first missionaries going
out in his name. It seems that Jesus prefers his missionaries to be poor
and without means to support themselves. Why? Perhaps to encourage
greater faith. Perhaps to allow him the opportunity to provide for those
he calls. Whatever the reason, this is how he dealt with Faustina. Luckily,
Faustina did not have to face her parents directly in this moment. She
was living apart from them in Łódź and was working as a domestic
servant. Her father's cousin, Michael Rapacki, had given her lodging.
She did not tell him much of her plans or the reasoning behind them,
only stopping long enough to say goodbye. She hinted to her sister a
little of what she was experiencing in her soul and where she was going.
Taking only the dress she was wearing, Faustina left for Warsaw at the
age of eighteen. She had no other belongings, no money, no food. She
somehow managed to procure a train ticket to Warsaw, a city where
Faustina knew not a single person. She trusted solely in her Lord.

One can imagine that as she left, all that is familiar about her passes away. Her life is taking a drastic turn and will never be the same. Jesus tends to cross our paths in this way. Not much is clear other than the call itself. We must allow the old familiar securities of life to fade away and allow a new life in Christ to begin.

Traveling into the unknown is never easy. Moving to a new city, starting a new job, getting married—all of these decisions involve an initial resolve that must be renewed over and over and over again. In the same way, the first "yes" to Jesus, small at first, is only the beginning of many "yeses." With each response the invitation becomes deeper and more all-consuming. One "yes" becomes a lifetime of "yeses" down a road that could never be imagined from the humble beginnings. This is the poverty of Jesus that is, in reality, his greatest wealth. He strips himself, comes to us in poverty and in his sacred humanity, and invites us. Stripped bare and made poor, Jesus reveals his love for us by dying on a cross. He yearns for our response of love. This poor Nazorean will never stop loving us and will never stop calling us to share in his love. This truly is a poverty that must be shared.

THURSDAY OF THE FIRST WEEK OF LENT

TRUSTING THE BELOVED

"Truly I tell you, unless you change and become like children, you will never enter the kingdom of heaven. Whoever becomes humble like this child is the greatest in the kingdom of heaven."

MATTHEW 18:3–4

Readings from the **Diary**: *1700, 1701, 1824*

In Faustina's journey to live out God's holy will, she needed to trust Jesus in a radical way. This trust in Our Lord, even when one hesitates and is unsure, is a virtue that all Christians should try to foster in their own lives. Trusting in the Lord as little children was a direct invitation from our Lord in the above Gospel passage.

The Kingdom of Heaven is not like the kingdoms of the Earth. It cannot be taken or possessed, but rather it is gifted to those who are able to receive it, just as a child receives a gift without question. All of us, great and small, rich and poor, young and old, must develop an attitude of spiritual simplicity like that of a child. The Gospels contain many other analogies explaining the Kingdom of Heaven and how to enter it, but they all come down to this path of childlike simplicity.

Many wrestle with this paradox. It is much easier to rely on our own strength and security. We imagine that God needs our human qualities to do great things for him, when in reality he wants our

23

littleness. Becoming small like the child is often difficult and contrary to what society says will make us happy. Work harder, make more money, take more vacations, herald your own cause, purchase your own happiness, man up. . . . The attitude of a child who simply receives everything from their parents contradicts all that the world idolizes. It takes more bravery to let go of your security and plans and let God provide than doing it your own way. Spiritual courage is all too often lacking in those society would have us imitate.

A child, and therefore a childlike spirituality, has three characteristics:

1. *They are willing to be led anywhere.*
2. *They are willing to be taught anything.*
3. *They have a capacity to wonder at everything.*

Take the hand of any toddler, and as long as you are not a stranger, the child will walk with you wherever you go, with no worry about the destination. It is enough for a child to hold the hand of a parent; nothing else matters. It is only in later years that the child no longer wants to be led but wants to go in his or her own direction.

Children can also wonder in the deepest of ways. To wonder is to allow oneself to be awed by the mystery of God and his creation. Children ask why things are the way they are, and parents must deal with their endless questions. They want to know everything about the world around them, and they trust the answers of the adults in their lives without need of proof. This simplicity does not last. As the child grows, the need for proof and scientific facts also grows, and the ability to wonder begins to wane. The simple answers from childhood no longer suffice, and this spirit of simplicity often becomes a spirit of superiority as we start believing that we know more than others.

If God is to become our everything, we must leave behind the "adulthood" of self-sufficiency and autonomy. This is why it is important to become a child in the spiritual life and depend more and more on God each day. This seems contradictory to our human nature. We expect young adults to grow into self-sufficient individuals. The opposite is true of the spiritual life. True holiness is deep trust and dependence on God alone. We grow up biologically and walk on our own; we grow "small" spiritually when we learn to walk with God. Being a spiritual child—an invitation from Our Lord no less—does not mean that we stop thinking, choosing, discerning, and making free and loving decisions regarding our lives. We do all those things without losing the trustful and peaceful disposition of our soul before God.

St. Faustina's early life was a period of tempering that prepared her to receive the revelation of Divine Mercy. Her childhood, her call to religious life, her difficulties in finding a convent, and her intense suffering during her novitiate together became the spiritual journey that readied her soul to become the Apostle of Divine Mercy. Only after this preparation was Faustina ready to behold Jesus as he appeared to her in the now iconic Divine Mercy image.

FRIDAY OF THE FIRST WEEK OF LENT

ALONE IN WARSAW

The Lord passed before him, and proclaimed,
"The Lord, the Lord, a God merciful and gracious,
slow to anger, and abounding in steadfast love and faithfulness.
Exodus 34:6

Readings from the **Diary***: 11, 12, 1576*

Jesus called Faustina to spiritual childlikeness. All throughout the pages of her diary, he repeats over and over the need for her to trust him completely like a child in the arms of her Father. She would need this spiritual attitude very much as she stepped off the train at Warsaw.

> *She sobbed "until she shook," recalls Stanislava Rapacka*
> *(her aunt). Helen asked her uncle to take her to the train*
> *. . . Seated in the compartment, she still cried so hard that*
> *"it was painful to watch. If the train had stopped, I probably*
> *would have taken her off it. But it didn't stop," he later told*
> *his wife. Is this at all surprising? Helen was 19 years old. She*
> *was on a train to the unknown. She was following the voice*
> *of Jesus, to whom she entrusted herself completely.*[11]

---

11 Ewa Czaczkowska, *Faustina*, 72.

The train ride to Warsaw took two hours and twenty minutes. When she exited the train, it was already getting dark, and naturally Faustina was afraid. As she watched the other passengers leave and go about their business with purpose, she truly had no idea where to go next. Faustina was a lost young girl standing at a train station in Warsaw. No one paid her any attention. No one offered to help her.

It is in this moment, alone and afraid, that Faustina turned to Jesus and Mary for guidance. They did not fail her. Whether the words were spoken in her heart or out loud, she couldn't say, but Faustina felt directed to go outside of Warsaw to a certain village and there would find lodging. She obeyed and found everything exactly as she heard.

The next morning, Faustina retraced her steps and entered a church she had passed the night before. The church was dedicated to the Immaculate Conception. Faustina spent some time in prayer and then attended the daily Mass. The pastor of the church was Fr. James Dabrowski, and Faustina felt Jesus tell her to share everything with this priest (*Diary*, 12). After Mass, Faustina approached Fr. James and opened her heart to him.

At first, Fr. James was very surprised, but he quickly seemed to know exactly what to do. In this moment, Fr. James must have had in mind two things. First, Faustina was obviously poor, alone, and in need of help. Second, she needed time to find a congregation of religious sisters who would accept her. After listening to Faustina and encouraging her to trust in God, Fr. James sent her to Aldona, a pious old lady of the parish who was looking for some domestic help. Fr. James knew that Aldona would welcome Faustina into her home. There Faustina found lodging until she could find a proper convent for herself.

Here begins a year and a half of waiting for Faustina, and during this time of waiting, she learns another lesson in the spiritual life. At the festival dance, Jesus came to Faustina urgently imploring her to decide how she would live her life, and in response she set off in haste to Warsaw. This "urgency" of Christ, however, was not for her to arrive at the end of her spiritual journey, but for her to begin it. Jesus takes his time in his work of sanctification, and we must let Jesus take his time with us, even if this seems harder than the actual path we walk.

A spiritual person allows God to act, just as a child allows and trusts its parents to act. The sin of spiritual wrath is to be impatient with God and impatient with oneself. It is a roadblock and an obstacle that all of us must overcome.

Faustina first imagined that she would quickly join a religious congregation, and she did not even consider that a year would go by before she would be admitted. Yet the paradox is this: her time of waiting and longing became clay in the hands of God. Not being able to act formed her in holiness more than if she had been able to do as she pleased.

SATURDAY OF THE FIRST WEEK OF LENT

A SYNTHESIS OF THE LIFE OF JESUS

For I desired mercy, and not sacrifice: and the
knowledge of God more than holocausts.
—*Hosea 6:6 (DRA)*

Readings from the **Diary***: 528, 582, 587, 1578*

After Faustina arrived in Warsaw, she would spend a year in preparation for her entrance to religious life. Faustina was alone and beginning a new life of union with God that could not have been easy to embrace. It must have been a lonely time for her. She was not with her family or friends, and she did not have a clear understanding of her life's next steps. Perhaps unknown to Faustina, Jesus was calmly working deep within her heart and soul. She was learning to be like Jesus.

The Lord Jesus lived out a deeply trusting relationship to the Father. A central part of the revelation that Christ made to us is that Jesus taught his disciples to call God "Father" (Matthew 6:5–8). This daring statement got Jesus into trouble with the Pharisees on different occasions. When speaking to an authority figure such as a judge or a teacher, we tend to speak with a formalized tone, but the tone of a child to a loving father is completely different. This change of tone reveals a change of essence. If the motor of my prayer life is love, I run to prayer, to my Father, because of love. If my motor is obedience, need, want, or fear, those attitudes will pervade my very conversation with God.

To call God Father is to restore to him the place he desires, the place of Fatherhood that was lost in Genesis. God can do all things without our aid, yet he chooses to want to work through us. In return, let us give God the place of Father in our lives by giving him our love and trust. Indeed, only we can give him the fatherhood he desires. By addressing God as Father in prayer, we allow ourselves to be immersed in a conversation of love. And so the prayer of Jesus, at its core, is simply loving God as his very own child. It is a tender, gentle, joyful and thankful prayer.

The prayer of Jesus to the Father was also existential, dealing with his real-life events and the state of his being as it truly was. Existential prayer is prayer that comes from the heart and flows into the Heart of God. In the Garden of Gethsemane, Jesus did not have an easy time of it. He came before God as he was, not someone he pretended to be. The Father meets the Son wherever the Son is. Prayer that is overly static and formal is not as connected to our daily life. Our prayer should pass through our heart, our daily life and situation. If we present ourselves before God only in specific and measured ways, we are hiding behind a mask. Jesus teaches us to come as we are and speak to him about the day-to-day things that affect us. God loves our humanity.

Jesus' life with his Father was also hidden. Jesus does not purposely try to hide his prayer from others; in fact, there are moments when it seems he makes a point to pray in front of large crowds. His intention is not to hide from others, but to go find God in silence and simplicity. He went out into the night to find God. He went out into the desert and to the mountaintop to find God. Each moment of prayer becomes a pilgrimage toward the Divine, which is such a splendid image of the soul seeking God.

Every time Jesus prayed, the apostles took note of the time, the place, his attitude, his emotions. They discovered these characteristics of the prayer of Jesus firsthand, and they documented them, spoke of them, and above all learned from them. The apostles realized that prayer was not something done only in the Temple or the synagogue, but prayer was a way of life. Faustina would find comfort in this heart of Jesus, a place of refuge. Faustina would eventually say that her soul was like a large and magnificent world for her and God to dwell alone (*Diary*, 582). This aloneness with God became a gift, perhaps difficult at first, but over time, Faustina welcomed this new way of life.

SECOND SUNDAY OF LENT

THE PATRON SAINT OF IMPERFECT DISCERNMENT

Mercy draws good from evil. It is the love that does not allow itself to be conquered by evil, pain, or suffering, but overcomes evil with good. Jesus took on, in his burning love for us, our entire human existence, in order to redeem it. He became flesh so that our flesh could become him.

SR. MARIE VERITAS, SV[12]

Readings from the Diary: *13, 56, 574, 699*

The term *discernment* in Catholic parlance connotes a process or method to decide upon a particular path or decision in light of God's will. Discernment was central to the teaching of St. Ignatius of Loyola. He developed a long retreat called the Spiritual Exercises that would aid a person to discern God's will in their lives. A person seeking to make a change or grow in their spiritual life would spend a month or so in prayer, contemplating different truths of the faith. Eventually, through spiritual direction and attention to the interior movements of the soul, they would come to a better understanding of what God was asking them.

Faustina did not go through a formal process of discernment. She had little education and no spiritual director. She did not know what to do next but allowed herself to be led each day. Faustina had no guides,

---

12 Sr. Marie Veritas, SV, *Beautiful Mercy*, 81.

no instruction—she was alone. In her simplicity she let Jesus do her discernment for her.

We can unofficially call St. Faustina the patron saint of imperfect discernment! Here was her process: After arriving in Warsaw, Faustina simply knocked on the first convent she could find, knowing nothing of the congregation itself, and asked admittance. If she was turned away, she continued to find the next one. We could possibly call this discernment by the process of elimination.

Anyone today discerning a religious vocation—men and women alike—are encouraged to study the congregation they seek to enter and learn about its charism and apostolic works, its rules and norms. In addition, they should spend time as a guest in that community, trying out the lifestyle. All of the knowledge, experiences, and personal prayer is then brought before a spiritual director, and through guidance of the Holy Spirit, a person makes their decision.

Faustina did none of this. She blindly trusted that Jesus would lead her where he wanted. Faustina placed her discernment in the hands of Jesus and, while her discernment seems imperfect by our standards today, it was more than adequate. She was willing to be led, and Jesus did not lead her astray.

The congregation that Faustina finally entered did not really suit her well. Faustina desired time for prayer, but instead she found much hard work and little time for prayer. Her congregation was based on a Jesuit-style prayer life where prayer and action intertwine, but Faustina was more like a Carmelite; she was a contemplative at heart. While Faustina was overjoyed to have finally entered a convent, she often felt like a stranger within her new family.

The simplicity and trust of Faustina were some of her greatest virtues. Jesus began forming these traits in her soul from the very beginning, all in preparation for the coming mission of being the Apostle of Divine Mercy.

Faustina left her old self behind when she gave God control of her life. Her discernment, more than analyzing her heart and life experiences, was to follow wherever her Beloved led. If he went left, she went left. If right, then to the right she would go. Through her obedience, Faustina made all the right decisions, not because she figured them out on her own, but because she trusted that God knew what he was doing. Faustina wanted only to find Jesus, and her search for him, which began at a dance in Łódź, lasted her whole lifetime.

MONDAY OF THE SECOND WEEK OF LENT

SEEKING THE BRIDEGROOM IN WARSAW

*I will rise, and will go about the city: in the streets and the broad ways
I will seek him whom my soul loveth: I sought him, and I found him not.*
SONG OF SONGS 3:2

Readings from the **Diary**: *1690, 1705, 1784*

Catholic theology draws heavily on Sacred Scripture for its most beloved analogies of the spiritual life. One of the most well-known and well-loved images is that of the bride and Bridegroom from the Song of Songs. This image is used often to speak of the relationship between a soul and Our Lord, or between the Church and Our Lord. Jesus is the Bridegroom, and each individual Christian is the bride. The bride (the soul) is sought by the Bridegroom (Christ). The bride, in turn, begins to seek after the beloved Bridegroom. This image of the searching bride is one of the best analogies we have to understand the nature of Christian perfection.

In Faustina's personal journey, she was blessed with an immense desire to pursue the Beloved. Her life ultimately became a continual search for Jesus. The journey was often a lonely one made through unfamiliar territory, but she knew in whose footsteps she followed. None of her fellow community sisters ever knew fully of her tryst with Divine Mercy. Only a handful of her superiors even understood that

35

something special was happening within her soul. Faustina shared her inner journey only with Jesus and her confessor. And while we are able to accompany her through her diary, it is only at a distance. In a sense, we each must embrace our own journey. No two journeys will be exactly the same.

The above passage from the Song of Songs expresses a common experience of the spiritual life. We set off on a journey toward heaven, following the footsteps of Christ. Our pilgrimage brings us many experiences, some good and some bad. Sometimes we walk in the light of day and sometimes in the dark of night. We seek to discover the Beloved, but he is not always immediately recognizable. The goal of this journey is the embrace of the Beloved, of heaven itself, yet sometimes it seems we must say with the Song of Songs, "I found him not." Faustina will spend a good amount of time seeking out Jesus in Warsaw, and at times she probably felt like the bride, saying to herself after a long day, "I sought him, and I found him not."

In the Song of Songs, we find the bride lying on her bed as night falls and the darkness creeps in. She lies awake listening for the Bridegroom, attentive to his coming. The Bridegroom comes softly and quietly to her door and peers into her room. When he sees her, he knocks and waits for her answer. The Bridegroom beautifully embodies the ways of Christ, who comes often to the door of our hearts in unexpected and unpredictable ways.

The Song of Songs depicts our earthly spiritual journey, not life in our final heavenly destination. Our human weaknesses walk with us throughout this journey, and the bride in the Song of Songs is no exception. She hesitates for a moment before opening the door, and when she does, she finds that the Bridegroom is gone. Thus begins a game of divine hide-and-seek. The Bridegroom is not gone from her life, but rather he is inviting her to find him. And so the bride steps out into the darkness to pursue her Love. She chases after the sound of his footsteps and is led to the trysting place. On her journey she walks through the city streets and countryside seeking him out. She catches brief glimpses of him, which serve to encourage her in her search. Finally she finds him, and together they enter the secret garden.

Anyone who has embarked on a life of prayer will experience this divine game of hide-and-seek. It is a multifaceted experience of desiring, wanting, and yearning—at times possessing him and at times feeling abandoned by him. There are exhilarating moments of climbing high up the mountains and other disconcerting moments of descending down into the valley, searching among the brambles and through thickets for Jesus. The good and bad blend together into a progressive whole that is our life's journey, which finds its ultimate fulfillment in heaven.

TUESDAY OF THE SECOND WEEK OF LENT

WALKING ALONE WITH JESUS

The messianic message of Christ and His activity among people end with the cross and resurrection. We have to penetrate deeply into this final event–which especially in the language of the Council is defined as the Mysterium Paschale—if we wish to express in depth the truth about mercy, as it has been revealed in depth in the history of our salvation.

St. John Paul II[13]

Readings from the **Diary***: 83, 148, 1588*

Faustina was no stranger to journeying alone. Even as a child she shared an intimacy with Jesus that seemed to set her apart. A neighbor reported that one day she saw young Faustina walking home from church alone; it was the day of her First Communion. When asked why she was walking by herself, Faustina told her neighbor, "I am walking with the Lord Jesus."[14] In fact, from the day of her First Communion on, she would return from Church alone, not conversing with the other girls her age so she could speak with Jesus present in her heart. A very real relationship with Jesus was blossoming in her heart. Jesus was never just a thought or idea to Faustina; he was as real as anyone else in her life.

---

13 St. John Paul II, *Dives in Misericordia*, 7; https://www.vatican.va/content/john-paul-ii/en/encyclicals/documents/hf_jp-ii_enc_30111980_dives-in-misericordia.html.
14 Ewa Czaczkowska, *Faustina*, 42.

Throughout her diary, Faustina displays an intense desire for Christ that made her behave in ways that might seem extreme even to someone dedicated to spiritual growth. At times she would wait at the door of the convent just to catch a glimpse of the poor who would come and go in order that she might see Jesus in them. She often rose in the middle of the night to pray in the chapel. She narrates that once she awoke in the night to discover that her clock had stopped. Afraid that she might oversleep and miss Holy Mass, she immediately got up and walked to the church. She arrived so early that the church was still locked, but she waited outside for hours until the door was opened (see *Diary*, 826). Perhaps this behavior seems like madness, but for Faustina, it was an expression of the deepest love for her Beloved. No sacrifice is too much for love, and Faustina spared no sacrifice in her search for Jesus. This can be a description of a saint—someone who never stops looking for Jesus. As Faustina's life progressed, she desired less and less anything of this world and sought only Jesus.

While Faustina was in Warsaw, but before she was accepted into a convent, we can imagine her walking home from daily Mass as she had ever since her First Communion, alone with Jesus. Every day as she walked, she kept her eyes and heart open to catch a glimpse of that secret trysting place Christ was preparing for her. There was great sorrow in her search as the days and months passed and she returned to the home of Aldona empty-handed. Yet there were joys, too, as each new day brought new hope that she might find him.

Faustina's life reveals the agony and the ecstasy of her search for Jesus. The more she sought and was rejected, the greater her desire for the Beloved grew. She suffered, but in her suffering God made her trysting place all the more beautiful and ready for her arrival.

WEDNESDAY OF THE SECOND WEEK OF LENT

AN UNSUITABLE CANDIDATE

In the eschatological fulfillment mercy will be revealed as love, while in the temporal phase, in human history, which is at the same time the history of sin and death, love must be revealed above all as mercy and must also be actualized as mercy. Christ's messianic program, the program of mercy, becomes the program of His people, the program of the Church. At its very center there is always the cross, for it is in the cross that the revelation of merciful love attains its culmination.

ST. JOHN PAUL II[15]

Readings from the **Diary***: 92, 133*

We have already mentioned why Faustina was not a prime candidate to be accepted into a convent, but to understand her journey with greater clarity, it is worth examining in greater detail the great mountains that blocked Faustina's way.

The first major obstacle was her education. Faustina had attended only two years of formal schooling. This lack of education was a major obstacle for her. Most congregations wanted sisters who could read and write, who could be taught and themselves teach, sisters who could be leaders and helpers. Faustina was quick enough to learn, but her lack of formal education was a deal breaker for many convents.

---

15 St. John Paul II, *Dives in Misericordia*, 8.

The second obstacle was her extreme poverty. Faustina had almost no money or clothing and no dowry to speak of whatsoever. Her family was so poor that among her sisters, there was only one dress that was dignified enough to wear to Holy Mass. The girls took turns wearing the dress, and if it wasn't their turn to wear it, they stayed home. Thus, poverty sometimes kept Faustina away from church as a child, and now poverty kept her away from a convent as an adult. In addition, most convents asked potential candidates to provide money or material for the different articles of clothing a sister would wear, especially the religious habit. No convent would accept Faustina outright because she had no way to cover these expenses.

The third obstacle, and perhaps the most difficult to overcome, was that Faustina's story was not entirely believable. We don't know exactly what she told the superiors of each convent, but Faustina tended to be reserved about her mystical experiences. At that time in Poland and throughout the Church at large, hard work, discipline, and a virtuous life were valued far above the mystical. Effort and sacrifice were considered the proper means of sanctification, and any extraordinary event or mystical experience was viewed with suspicion. To present herself to the convents as a mystic, or anything other than primarily a hard worker in the spiritual life, would have marked Faustina as an undesirable or a least a suspicious candidate.

The last obstacle, but by no means the least, was that Faustina did not have permission from her family. Having her parents' blessing was not a formal requirement but was considered beneficial in the long-term, especially for the psychology of the young woman seeking entrance. As it stood, Faustina was only slightly above being a simple runaway. She was of age and could freely choose to give her life, but she certainly would never have an enticing dowry to present the convent. The most she could offer were the meager savings from her work as a domestic servant.

None of these realities weighed in on Faustina's decision to follow

God's call. She knew Jesus would take care of everything if she trusted in him. Her ignorance of the difficulties she would encounter when she commenced her search of Warsaw tested her faith like no other. Faustina sought after the Beloved, but he had vanished into the night. God seemed absent from Faustina during this period in her life. Again and again, she was rejected because of who she was and not valued for who she could become. And the trials of misunderstanding did not stop there. Aldona, the woman who had given lodging to Faustina, secretly began preparations to find Faustina a suitor.

Just as the bride in the Song of Songs, though, we see Faustina arise and search the streets and alleys for her trysting place. In a mysterious way, this search and suffering renders the bride even more beautiful and ready for the Bridegroom when she does find him.

THURSDAY OF THE SECOND WEEK OF LENT

THE TRYSTING PLACE AT LAST

Mercy is the very foundation of the Church's life. All of her pastoral activity should be caught up in the tenderness she makes present to believers; nothing in her preaching and in her witness to the world can be lacking in mercy. The Church's very credibility is seen in how she shows merciful and compassionate love.
POPE FRANCIS, *MISERICORDIA VULTUS*, [10]

Readings from the **Diary***: 1123, 14, 1760*

Nothing is too hard for love. No mountain is too high or desert too vast. As the spiritual life progresses, we should realize that discovery of the Beloved requires a commitment to reaching the depths of love. There are roads on the journey toward the Beloved that only one who loves can pass through. Faustina writes that love was all she needed; it solved every problem and crossed over every precipice (see *Diary*, 1123). This love for Jesus, in spite of the odds against her, eventually bore the desired fruit.

One day, as Faustina was reaching the end of her list, she arrived at the door of the Sisters of Our Lady of Mercy. To us, perhaps, the name of the congregation should have drawn Faustina's attention much sooner, but she was at the beginning of her journey with Divine Mercy and did not yet understand the role it was to play in her life. Clearly though, Jesus and Mary prepared the way for Faustina.

43

The sister in charge of the convent was Mother Michael Olga Moraczcewska. Faustina did not make much of an impression on her at first. Mother Michael had interviewed countless young women in similar situations. Through God's providence, however, something prompted Mother Michael to give Faustina a chance. Before she accepted Faustina, she sent her to the small chapel to ask Jesus, the "Lord of the House," if he would accept her.

The convent in Warsaw was not one large building, but rather a series of smaller buildings around a church. As the sisters had frequent need of praying before the Blessed Sacrament, and by their rule tried to live under the same roof as Jesus, they had permission to reserve the Eucharist on a second-floor room in their private home. Thus, they did not need to go to the church each time they were to visit Jesus. It was here to this chapel, hidden and tucked away within the convent walls, that Faustina was directed.

Faustina went alone to the small chapel and knelt before the tabernacle. Her long search for the Beloved was over. The trysting place she sought after for months turned out to be this little chapel on the second floor of the Congregation of Our Lady of Mercy. It was as if Faustina had climbed to that place higher up where the bride of the Song of Songs meets the Bridegroom in the cleft high in the rock (see Song of Songs 2:14). And as Faustina asked the Lord of this trysting place for acceptance, she heard Jesus speak to her heart: "I do accept; you are in my heart" (*Diary*, 14).

What joy and comfort these words of Jesus must have brought to the heart of Faustina! After searching for more than a year, living on faith alone, suffering through rejection after rejection, believing in her vocation while others conspired against her and tried to drag her back into the dance of the world—after all that—she had finally come home. It was an even more beautiful discovery to realize that, while the small convent she entered was where God wanted her, her true home was her place in the Sacred Heart of Jesus.

Often at the end of a period of hardship, we are tempted to look back over the road traveled and complain or wonder at the God who would lead us down such a path. Faustina could have easily done this as well. *Why, O Lord, did you let me suffer?*

The Beloved wants us to focus on him, not on the journey itself. We may never fully understand God's divine plan during this life on Earth. To demand answers and explanations about the passing moments on our journey is to lack trust. It also slows us down. Jesus is in a hurry! He is compelled by love, a love so great it wishes to draw all people to walk with him on this journey.

FRIDAY OF THE SECOND WEEK OF LENT

THE SAINTS OF DARKNESS

For unto you it is given for Christ, not only to
believe in him, but also to suffer for him.
PHILIPPIANS 1:29

Readings from the **Diary:** *95–97, 576, 691*

A common misconception in relation to the saints is that they all led beautiful lives and were filled with the constant and overwhelming presence of the love of God. They never wavered or doubted their calls. Every step was a sure one that led to a satisfied and happy life. All we have to do is look at the glowing and bright stained glass windows that decorate our churches to see the smiles and roses that embodies sanctity. If only our own lives could be so perfect!

However, to read the account of any real-life saint is a sobering reality. Gone is the beauty and perfection, to be replaced with a powerful conviction of God's love that keeps them afloat in a sea of doubt, suffering, and isolation. Saints are human. They walk in the darkness of faith the same as the rest of us; the difference is that they choose to live heroically by their faith.

A simple explanation of the life of a saint is a leaving behind of old ways of life in order to live the very life of Jesus. It is the aspiration of the apprentice or student seeking to walk in the footsteps of the master. To take on the life of Jesus, however, is no easy walk. Jesus left heaven to walk on the earth as a human, taking on the life of his own creatures. He left, so to speak, the eternal embrace of the Father to walk among us. We will never fully understand what this giving up of heaven entailed for Jesus. Yet we can suggest here a few thoughts about the life of Jesus. Jesus was drawn to the Father and longed for him with a love beyond all telling. It was this yearning for the Father that shaped the life of Jesus and expressed itself in his daily life and prayer. It was both a blessing and a suffering. For Jesus, this desire for the Father is what fueled his long nights of prayer and fasting. It was the purpose of his preaching and miracles; it was the reason for the depth of his sorrow when he wept on the hills overlooking Jerusalem and when he cried out "My God, my God, why have you forsaken me!" (Matthew 27:46). Much joy abounded in the life of Jesus, but equally a part of his life was this anguished yearning for the Father. This is the part that often only contemplative souls embrace. The mystical side of the Christian life is to walk with Jesus even on the difficult roads.

The spiritual life of St. Faustina was no different. When Jesus first appeared to her, it was not in the radiant and beautiful light of his Divine Mercy. He appeared as the suffering Savior on Calvary, seeking for someone to accompany him in his Passion. Faustina shows great courage to leave behind her entire world, her potential future, her family, and her comforts, all to take the hand of the Crucified One and walk where he led.

SATURDAY OF THE SECOND WEEK OF LENT

❦

THE "RELUCTANT" SAINT OF DIVINE MERCY

Mercy in itself, as a perfection of the infinite God, is also infinite. Also infinite therefore and inexhaustible is the Father's readiness to receive the prodigal children who return to His home. Infinite are the readiness and power of forgiveness which flow continually from the marvelous value of the sacrifice of the Son. No human sin can prevail over this power or even limit it. On the part of man only a lack of good will can limit it, a lack of readiness to be converted and to repent, in other words persistence in obstinacy, opposing grace and truth, especially in the face of the witness of the cross and resurrection of Christ.

St. John Paul II[16]

Readings from the **Diary**: *22, 135, 571*

When a young woman enters a congregation, she is not admitted immediately as a full-fledged member. The Church, in her wisdom, asks that this admittance process be gradual, allowing both the congregation and the one seeking admittance to get to know one another. This process looks different in each congregation and often has different stages leading up to full membership, also known as final vows. Across the board, however, is the initial stage known as candidacy or postulancy, during which a person lives the life of the order but has not taken any vows and does not wear any habit. Faustina did a few short months as

---

16 *Dives in Misericordia*, 13.

a candidate to her new order. Once this period of time was complete, a date was set for her to receive the religious habit and start the next stage of discernment as a novice of the congregation. The date chosen for her "clothing day," as it was affectionately called, was April 26, 1926.

The reception of the habit took place during Holy Mass. The atmosphere, while joyful at the reception of a new sister for the order, was also a reminder to the candidate of their choice to turn away from the world and enter into a life of self-denial for the sake of Jesus. The themes of this Mass are rich and beautiful, but also stark. On the one hand, it is funeral in that the candidate dies to the things of the world. On the other hand, it is a betrothal to the Beloved as the bride takes on a new life in Christ.

To aid the candidates through the ceremony, each is assigned to a senior sister who becomes a sort of sponsor to her, presenting her to the congregation as well as helping her into the habit. The sister assigned to Faustina was named Sr. Clemens. It is from Sr. Clemens that we have a description of Faustina as she received her habit. To the surprise of all the sisters, as soon as Faustina took the habit into her hands she grew faint, collapsed, and lay unmoving on the floor. Someone fetched smelling salts with which to revive Faustina. Once she was awake again and the ceremony could continue, everyone breathed a sigh of relief. They joked that Faustina was reluctant to leave the world behind!

We hear a completely different story from Faustina herself in her diary. She relates that the moment she received her habit, a moment that definitively set her apart from the world and marked her as belonging only to God, Jesus came to her and revealed to her all she was to suffer in her lifetime ahead. Her entry is unclear as to whether this was a vision or a mental image or pure knowledge, but from that point on she had a clear understanding of the depths of suffering she would undergo for the sake of his name.

It was the weight of this knowledge, not hesitancy to leave the world behind, that caused Faustina to collapse. Yet even with this knowledge, when Faustina recovered herself, she rose and put on the habit. This was her response to Jesus' invitation to walk the path of Calvary. As she donned this new attire and died to the world, Faustina, a new person, emerged. Gone was the innocent, naïve girl who stepped off the train in Warsaw. She knew the trials that lay ahead and embraced them, albeit with some trembling and fear. It was a new stage of faith—not one that trusted blindly, but one that walked with open eyes, and more importantly, with an accepting heart.

THIRD SUNDAY OF LENT

THE DARK NIGHT OF THE SOUL

One dark night,
fired with love's urgent longings
— ah, the sheer grace! —
I went out unseen,
my house being now all stilled.
. . . O guiding night!
O night more lovely than the dawn!
O night that has united
the Lover with his beloved,
transforming the beloved in her Lover.
St. John of the Cross, *The Dark Night*

Readings from the **Diary**: *1485, 1487*

The day Faustina received her habit marked the beginning of her novitiate, a two-year period of intense spiritual training and preparation before taking the religious vows of poverty, chastity, and obedience. During the novitiate, Faustina was free to leave the congregation at any time. It was a year into her novitiate that Faustina began to experience the suffering foretold her. This suffering came to her in April 1927, and she thus began her dark night of the soul.

The term *dark night of the soul* requires a brief explanation in order for us to understand and appreciate, even to a small extent, what Faustina went through. The term *dark night of the soul* is not just some poetic phrasing but was identified and coined by St. John of the Cross.

St. John of the Cross was a Spanish Carmelite and mystic who worked alongside St. Teresa of Avila. The two of them wrote extensively regarding the journey of a soul toward union with Christ. Both divide the spiritual life into a series of stages. For St. John of the Cross, the stages are a nighttime journey that ends with the sunrise. For St. Teresa of Avila, the stages are a progression through seven mansions inside an interior castle in the soul. Both explanations are meant to guide and provide milestones for the spiritual traveler, not a one-size-fits-all approach. As well, most spiritual authors suggest that we can go back and forth between the stages or be in multiple stages at once. Generally, a person who begins the spiritual journey must first turn away from the vices of the world. After these vices are uprooted from one's life, a soul then must acquire virtue. This arduous task is accomplished both through the efforts of the soul and the grace of God, although emphasis is placed on the work of God in us.

After growth in virtue comes a very important purification of the soul. There is the danger that the now virtuous soul can develop spiritual pride regarding their accomplishments. Happy with their progress, content with the consolations received in prayer, and satisfied with their reputation as a good and holy person, these well intending, spiritual people get trapped by their own virtue! They require deeper purification to be able to progress on the journey. The purification needed is for this person to completely lose all interest in self-advancement, all self-seeking in the spiritual life, all sense of personal accomplishment, and become utterly and totally dependent on God. In order for this to happen, the soul must be granted a full vision of itself in the truth of its own weakness and sin. Thus, a soul is rendered helpless so as to understand the depths of its own weakness. This is the process known as the dark night. Only in facing our true selves can we ever understand just how much we need God.

The dark night of the soul is unique to each person, as each of us has our own root sins, vices, and sources of pride. It could be called a "second conversion" that penetrates deeper, removing bad habits, fears, and compulsions by the roots. The fruit of the dark night experience is a selfless love, a faith transcending reason, and a spiritual hope that is not simply positive thinking but is grounded in the truth of heaven and God's eternal love for us.

This process is wrought by God alone. Unlike times of desolation or spiritual dryness that may come and go throughout one's life, the cause of this night of the soul is only God, and the end of the night comes only when God desires.

For Faustina, April 1927 ushered into her life the dark night of purification. It began with Faustina's understanding of God as a just judge. She felt a heaviness of heart and a despair that no matter what she did, before the eyes of the Judge, she could never be saved. Her prayer felt dry and empty. Her health was fragile. Above all, she did not experience the mercy of God but only his divine justice.

MONDAY OF THE THIRD WEEK OF LENT

✦

THE CHALICE OF THE BRIDEGROOM

At the very instant when Mary gave her consent, there took place the mystery
of the Incarnation- the union of the Divine Nature and the human nature
of Christ in one Divine Person, an act of the greatest possible Mercy, by
which Jesus began a new life, an act of eternal Mercy toward men, briefly
expressed in the words: "And the Word was made flesh and dwelt among us."
BL. MICHAEL SOPOCKO, 43

Readings from the Diary: 135, 136, 343

Faustina lists her sufferings and calls them a "cup of bitterness"
(Diary, 343). She recounts the loss of health and strength, fears and
bitterness, humiliations, false suspicions, terrors, dryness of spirit, fears
and incertitude, darkness and torments too difficult to describe. All
these descended upon her, and there seemed to be no escape. Yet Jesus
himself was the first to drink this cup of bitterness. He does not ask
of us anything that he himself has not suffered. Jesus offers this cup to
anyone willing to take it, as he said to James and John: "Are you able to
drink the cup that I am about to drink?" (Matthew 20:22).

Due to the suddenness with which these doubts and sufferings
came upon her, Faustina contemplated leaving the congregation.
Surely someone with this many problems could assume God was no
longer calling them to the religious life. It was only by God's grace

that she managed to finish that second year of novitiate. Faustina did not write much during this time, and so we can't piece together clearly just how she managed to continue forward. However, she recounts the experience in her diary years later, saying that the dark night came to an end around the same time she finished her novitiate. It went away gradually, unlike the suddenness with which it started.

Shortly after her purifying dark night experience, there came another crucial moment in her spiritual life. As she entered the chapel for adoration, God granted her another moment of spiritual clarity. All the aforementioned sufferings were presented to her, but this time they were to be suffered in the future. Faustina was asked to freely embrace the coming sufferings and to make herself a "sacrifice" to God. How close this experience was to what St. Paul invited every Christian to in his epistle to the Romans: "I appeal to you therefore, brothers and sisters, by the mercies of God, to present your bodies as a living sacrifice, holy and acceptable to God, which is your spiritual worship" (Romans 12:1).

In the spiritual life God always respects our freedom. This freedom is a gift, not a burden. Freedom enables us to truly love and to truly believe, without the use of force or coercion. The unique path of suffering that God laid out before Faustina was an offering; a free gift to her that she could take or leave without consequences.

Faustina chose to accept this gift and all the suffering it would entail. It was not done out of some masochistic desire, but out of love for God and for others. In the spiritual life, we call someone who, out of love, chooses to embrace suffering for the good of others a victim-soul. It is embracing the suffering of the cross above and beyond what is ordinarily asked. It is helping others to carry their crosses while carrying the full weight of one's own. Illness, suffering, imprisonment, and persecution seem to follow these souls to an unbelievable degree, yet all of these struggles and more are offered up to God in order to win graces for the Church. This is mystical theology at its highest.

Faustina freely chose to become a victim-soul. She understood her vocation as a call to suffer alongside the Bridegroom. She endured what Jesus endured: a longing for the Father to an insatiable degree that every action becomes a holocaust of love meant to draw more people to heaven.

TUESDAY OF THE THIRD WEEK OF LENT

THE CHURCH OF MERCY AS A FIELD HOSPITAL

Once you were not a people, but now you are God's people;
once you had not received mercy, but now you have received mercy.
1 Peter 2:10

Readings from the Diary: 146, 147, 742

In Pope Francis' second homily as pope he said: "Jesus has this message for us: mercy. I think—and I say it with humility—that this is the Lord's most powerful message: mercy" (March 17, 2013). Pope Francis is certainly a pope of mercy. He reflects on how the Church must enter into the world of today. For Pope Francis, the world today is a battlefield. The human person is abused and destroyed in countless ways never seen before. The war of good and evil, of life against death that is raging all around us, means that the Church must become more of a field hospital.

> *The Church does not exist to condemn people but to bring*
> *about an encounter with the visceral love of God's mercy.*
> *I often say that in order for this to happen, it is necessary*
> *to go out: to go out from the church and the parishes, to*
> *go outside and look for people where they live, where they*
> *suffer, and where they hope. I like to use the image of a*

field hospital to describe this "Church that goes forth";
it exists where there is combat, it is not a solid structure
with all the equipment where people go to receive
treatment for both small and large infirmities. It is a
mobile structure that offers first aid and immediate care,
so that its soldiers do not die. It's a place for urgent care,
not a place to see a specialist.[17]

Christ is the answer the entire world is looking for. He is the message itself—his very person. The desires of our hearts are ultimately personal, not theoretical. The answer we seek is not primarily a thought or an idea; first of all, we are seeking a love. This love is Christ, and that is why every apostle of Divine Mercy is a person deeply in love with the Lord. Transmitting love is done with the heart, not with the mind. The Church must be always ready to bring this mercy to wherever sin is found. Many people today, because of the epic dimensions of sin in the world, are no longer even able to knock on the Church door. They are in the street and do not even know that the Church is a place they can go to. Therefore a mobile Church, a Church in the streets to which they can go, is necessary for today. This doesn't mean closing up churches and standing in the streets. While it may mean this in some circumstances, above all it is an attitude, a change of paradigm. The Church will always be more than just a field hospital. She is a place of refuge, a bulwark of God's grace withstanding the passage of time. But she must also be in search of the lost sheep. This is what Pope Francis is inviting the Church as a whole to recover, her role as shepherd seeking out the lost sheep.

When Christ was preaching to his disciples, he used parables in order to convey divine truths. Of his many parables, perhaps the one that stands out the most is the story of the Prodigal Son. It touches us deeply because the depths of sin and despair of the son echo the feelings that most of us at some point have experienced. Thus, the parable is so

17 Pope Francis, *The Name of God Is Mercy* (New York: Random House, 2016).

effective because it speaks so directly to our human hearts. The story of the Prodigal Son should be a model for the Church herself, who, as Mother and Father, must speak to the hearts of her children. In it is expressed the truth that "only he who has been touched and caressed by the tenderness of his mercy really knows the Lord. For this reason I have often said that the place where my encounter with the mercy of Jesus takes place is my sin."[18]

---

18 Pope Francis, *The Name of God Is Mercy*.

WEDNESDAY OF THE THIRD WEEK OF LENT

A CALL WITHIN A CALL

Among the spiritual confusions of the current day, unfortunately, a misunderstanding of divine mercy is high on the list. For many people, God's mercy has shifted from divine forgiveness offered to the repentant sinner to a divine pity for the sinner who persists in sin and seems unable to extricate himself from his sin. In this understanding, mercy is directed primarily, not at the forgiveness of particular sins, but at the painful sense of guilt for sin. The sin itself is a secondary consideration, while mercy is somewhat like a spiritual blanket covering the soul with the warmth of divine compassion. Receiving mercy in this view does not at all require a struggle to overcome sin. Instead, it has become akin to an act of amnesty, a divine reprieve granted to a guilty conscience. It simply releases a soul from the burden of shame felt after committing sin. [...] a soft, indulgent notion of God's love for sinners takes hold, that God is all merciful and non-judgmental in a general way, an avuncular figure instead of a true father, winking a blind eye at the misfortune of grave transgressions.

Fr. Donald Haggerty[19]

Readings from the Diary: *824, 1804, 1385*

---

19 Fr. Donald Haggerty, *Conversion: Spiritual Insights into an Essential Encounter with God* (San Francisco: Ignatius Press, 2017), 75.

St. Faustina received a call within a call. The more Faustina listened to the heart of Jesus, the more she realized that she was not only called to be a sister of Our Lady of Mercy, but that she had a particular mission within her larger vocation as a religious sister: a call within a call. Her particular call was a call to suffering, to be a holocaust of love to God. In her diary (824), Faustina makes are veiled comments about a secret shared between her and Jesus. She says that nobody, and not even the angels will know this secret. It is a mystery that distinguishes her soul from all other.

We should not pretend to know or understand this secret, yet in the context of her life, this mystery of Faustina and Jesus possibly may have included a union in suffering. Jesus often requested her accompaniment in his Passion, and she was ever willing to take some of his suffering in her own life. Jesus had already suffered historically, but time and again Jesus has revealed to his saints the reality of suffering mystically. This mystical suffering of Faustina was highly valued by Jesus.

This passage in her diary gives us a brief glimpse into the hidden life of Faustina that no one, not even her confessor, was privy to. The secrecy of this mystery is essentially the intimacy between lovers, between a bride and bridegroom. The Christian life has the capacity to enter into this realm, drinking of the same chalice and sharing the same life as Jesus. How hard it is for us to imagine such intimacy with someone we cannot physically touch, see, or speak with! It is completely foreign to us and because of that, we sometimes seek to keep it at arm's length. When we do this, the mystical life remains a closed door, a mountain we may never climb. Suffering, the dark night, and purifications are all necessary elements if we are to lean our heads upon the bosom of Jesus. They are also free gifts. At some point in every Christian's life, God will offer these gifts. The depth and beauty of our spiritual life hinges upon our response to these gifts.

Suffering and advancement in the spiritual life go hand in hand. One calls mysteriously to the other. Often, suffering will lead a soul to spend more time before the Eucharist in adoration. Thus, the two earthly realities that are the envy of the angels come together: suffering and the Eucharist (see *Diary*, 1804). The reality of a suffering soul before the Eucharist is a blessed soul. And this is why St. John the Apostle, resting on the heart of Jesus, a form of Eucharistic adoration, enabled St. John to be the only apostle at the foot of the cross.

THURSDAY OF THE THIRD WEEK OF LENT

THE MOST PLEASING SOUL

No one has greater love than this, to lay down one's life for one's friends.
JOHN 15:13

Readings from the Diary*: 279, 1537, 1449*

To truly love someone means you want to give them the best of your love. No one aspires to love less than their beloved loves them. In a sense, being a "failure in love" is OK. To fail in love means in a sense to never be content with the amount of love you have shown toward God, a spouse, or a close relative. It means to wish to do more and not be content with giving another the crumbs of our love.

A Christian who is serious about the spiritual life seeks to return love for love, to love Christ as deeply as he loves us. For this reason, we should aspire to a crucified love, so that we can give without measure and willingly shoulder any difficulty for the sake of the Beloved. In her diary, Jesus made known to Faustina that a soul who embraces suffering and offers it as a fragrant incense to heaven is the soul that is most pleasing to him (see *Diary*, 279).

As two hearts learn to beat together, what pleases one slowly becomes what pleases the other. In her later life, Faustina discovered this joy in suffering and fostered it in her heart. She desired to joyfully drink from the chalice of the Beloved. She even thanks Our Lord for the cup of suffering in her daily life (see *Diary*, 1449).

Jesus also wanted her to accompany him in his mystical Passion.

> *During Holy Hour today, Jesus complained to me about the ingratitude of souls: In return for My blessings, I get ingratitude. In return for My love, I get forgetfulness and indifference. My Heart cannot bear this.* (*Diary*, 1537)

This is not the comment of an indifferent, untouchable God, but of a God of mercy and love who longs for his children with the love of a father.

When someone can smile from their own cross, as did Faustina, they are able to receive the most precious gifts of the spiritual life: to look in the mirror and see in their own reflection the face of Jesus smiling back. Hidden behind this smile is an entire world of love and beauty that is only seen through eyes of faith and hearts of love.

FRIDAY OF THE THIRD WEEK OF LENT

SETTING OUT FOR UNCHARTED SPIRITUAL LANDS

"Go and learn what this means, 'I desire mercy, not sacrifice.'
For I have come to call not the righteous but sinners."
Matthew 9:13

Readings from the Diary: *150, 201, 797*

History is defined not only by people and events but by the ideologies and philosophies of the times. Church history is no different, except in place of ideologies, we speak of the undercurrents of theology. It is these trends and developments in the theological mindset that often become the internal motors behind events. To understand the significance of Faustina and Divine Mercy, we must look behind the scenes to the theological thoughts of the times. Faustina was not claiming anything entirely new by promoting God's mercy. This was clearly a part of the spiritual patrimony of the Church from apostolic times. Yet as the times of history come and go, many original insights in the Gospels can become forgotten or overlooked.

Having no formal schooling or theological training, the little theology Faustina knew came from the preaching she heard in retreats, homilies, the advice of her confessors, and the spiritual reading she would do throughout her day. Many of these priests were Jesuits, men of solid learning and piety. Their ideals, founded by Ignatius of Loyola and tested and refined over centuries of missions, martyrs, controversies, and fidelity to the Holy See, helped shape the Polish clergy. These priests were accustomed to personal hardship and suffering, building and rebuilding their small churches and schools, as well enduring government persecutions. Theirs was a spirituality focused on hard work done for the glory of God and a daily examination of conscience to better discern the movements of the Spirit in their life and mission, on daily meditation, the proper use of creatures, opting for Christ, and ending in divine love.

In some ways it is remarkable that a young woman like Faustina brought such a spiritual renewal to the Church. There was nothing initially apparent about Faustina at first glance that would give any indication of her unique road ahead. While desiring nothing more than to conform and find a place to fit in, Faustina inadvertently questioned and challenged the accepted some of the spiritual currents of the times.

As regards to the Jesuit spirituality of the time, Faustina perhaps could have been initially better suited for a cloistered life of prayer. She seems to have resonated with a more Carmelite spirit. Even Faustina's poetry and writings reflected more the teachings and style of St. John of the Cross and Teresa of Ávila, both Carmelite reformers. Faustina also nurtured a great devotion to St. Thérèse of Lisieux, a French Carmelite sister and future Doctor of the Church. St. Thérèse herself brought a very novel "little way" into the spiritual life of the Church, shirking the more pessimistic and harsh ascetical tones of her French Catholic upbringing. Thérèse and Faustina were kindred spirits.

The Jesuit spirituality clearly fed the soul of Faustina and aided her throughout her life. But perhaps Faustina's leanings toward Carmelite spirituality is why it took so long for her to feel completely at home in her congregation. The daily schedule did not give her enough time for the prayer she yearned for. At the beginning of her religious life, Faustina gives the impression of enduring life in her community as opposed to thriving in it. Later on, she overcame these early difficulties and loved her congregation so much she could not bear the thought of leaving it.

SATURDAY OF THE THIRD WEEK OF LENT

FAUSTINA'S OUTWARD JOURNEY TO 1931

We need constantly to contemplate the mystery of mercy. It is a wellspring of joy, serenity, and peace. Our salvation depends on it. Mercy: the word reveals the very mystery of the Most Holy Trinity. Mercy: the ultimate and supreme act by which God comes to meet us. Mercy: the fundamental law that dwells in the heart of every person who looks sincerely into the eyes of his brothers and sisters on the path of life. Mercy: the bridge that connects God and man, opening our hearts to the hope of being loved forever despite our sinfulness.
POPE FRANCIS, *MISERICORDIA VULTUS*[2]

Readings from the **Diary**: *91, 146, 147*

Let us bring ourselves up to speed to 1931, the year of Faustina's first vision of Divine Mercy. In 1926 Faustina entered her congregation and began the prayer and hard work of a novice in her order. After two years she made her first vows of poverty, chastity, and obedience. For the next five years, Faustina would renew these vows and continue preparing herself in anticipation of the moment when she would be permitted to take her final vows. Shortly after her novitiate, she began working in different houses owned by the congregation, almost always assigned to kitchen duties or work in the fields and garden.

We spoke earlier of the difficulty Faustina faced when she first entered the convent based solely on her social status. Little did she know that this bias against her poor background would cling to her even as a professed sister. Among the sisters, there was a clear distinction that might seem unbelievable to us today but was very common for the time. When a woman entered the convent, those who were educated or came from wealthy and noble families joined what was known as the First Choir sisters. A woman who had no education or came from a poorer social background joined a lesser section of sisters called the Second Choir. From that moment on they were virtually separated into two classes. The First Choir sisters were given more education and set on the path to become superiors and future leaders of the congregation. The Second Choir sisters became their assistants, the ones who cooked and cleaned and kept the congregation functioning. The First Choir sisters received golden rings when they made their final profession of vows, while the Second Choir sisters received silver rings.

For obvious reasons, Faustina was sorted into the Second Choir. For her, the silver ring on her hand was not only a reminder of her espousal to Christ, but also of her humble condition. Knowing the history and practice of the time, it should not surprise us, then, that there was heavy jealousy and skepticism toward Faustina from those who could not fathom any sister outside the first choir to be chosen for a special mission and relationship with Jesus. Faustina was ridiculed as a hysteric and fanatic rather than treated with respect.

This, then, is the outward journey of Faustina from a poor young farm girl to a simple and humble religious sister in 1931. She was stripped of all things: her family and friends, the control she thought she had over her life—even her dream of what she thought religious life would be like was met with contradiction. Faustina was very much alone spiritually and emotionally. Jesus had brought her to a desert place, and there alone with him, Faustina was ready to meet the merciful Jesus.

FOURTH SUNDAY OF LENT

FAUSTINA'S INWARD JOURNEY TO 1931

The works of mercy are charitable actions by which we come to the aid of our neighbor in his spiritual and bodily necessities. Instructing, advising, consoling, comforting are spiritual works of mercy, as are forgiving and bearing wrongs patiently. The corporal works of mercy consist especially in feeding the hungry, sheltering the homeless, clothing the naked, visiting the sick and imprisoned, and burying the dead.

CATECHISM OF THE CATHOLIC CHURCH, 2447

Readings from the **Diary***: 56, 580, 651, 1160*

Christian living is fundamentally sacramental. We center our lives around the sacred and the veiled, and it is only natural that we, too, should become outward signs of inward realities. Outwardly Faustina was stripped of all her securities until it seemed nothing remained. This exterior reality veiled the more significant interior reality of her deep spiritual poverty.

Faustina's sudden departure from the world and acceptance into the humble Second Choir brought darkness to her soul along with many humiliations. While she never felt as close to God as when she answered his call into the religious life, she never felt so insecure. The joy of following Jesus seemed overshadowed by the many things he asked of her, many of which were new and frightening.

As she started the novitiate, her intense interior spiritual battles began. This dark night took the form of desolation and abandonment by God in prayer and was complemented by continual external humiliations by her sisters. Faustina was very afraid, and her fears and interior darkness threatened to consume her.

Faustina makes a curious statement regarding her preparation for mercy in her diary (see Diary, 56). She came to understand that for her to understand the greatness of God's mercy, she needed to experience the greatness of human misery. By hitting rock bottom, as the saying goes, Faustina knew then just how much she, and in turn all of humanity, truly needed a Savior. The darkness of Faustina's external journey was reflected in the darkness of her interior journey. Both had a purpose and place in the overall story of her life. Both were forging and grounding her in the mercy of Jesus.

This long and quiet preparation of Faustina follows a pattern seen first in the life of Our Lord. Jesus chose to live thirty quiet years on Earth before he said or did anything extraordinary. He need not have waited so long to begin his public ministry. Thus, his actions give us a lesson as to the meaning of our own simple lives on Earth. Jesus lived in the present, in the here and now. He was content to live under the roof of Mary as a simple carpenter obeying his mother and serving the people of Nazareth.

The tendency of our lives is to live looking for the next best thing. We look forward to graduating, to beginning our careers, to starting a family. Everything becomes about tomorrow and tomorrow and tomorrow. This obsession with the future pulls our eyes and heart away from the present moment. It is in the here and now that we become saints, not tomorrow and not yesterday. Jesus' waiting and patience in Nazareth is a lesson in humility. Living life in the present moment allows us to find the peace of God in the present day.

MONDAY OF THE FOURTH WEEK OF LENT

THE DIVINE MERCY REVELATION

*With our eyes fixed on Jesus and his merciful gaze, we experience the love
of the Most Holy Trinity. The mission Jesus received from the Father was
that of revealing the mystery of divine love in its fullness. "God is love" (1
Jn 4:8,16), John affirms for the first and only time in all of Holy Scripture.
This love has now been made visible and tangible in Jesus' entire life. His
person is nothing but love, a love given gratuitously. The relationships he forms
with the people who approach him manifest something entirely unique and
unrepeatable. The signs he works, especially in favour of sinners, the poor,
the marginalized, the sick, and the suffering, are all meant to teach mercy.
Everything in him speaks of mercy. Nothing in him is devoid of compassion.*
POPE FRANCIS, *MISERICORDIA VULTUS*, 8

Readings from the **Diary***: 186, 1032, 1777*

It was Sunday, February 22, 1931, in the dead of winter. Faustina had
been assigned to the convent in the town of Plock, and she spent most
of her time working in the kitchen bakery.

Faustina had finished her work and prayers for the day and was in
her room preparing for bed. It was in this moment that the merciful
Jesus first appeared to her. Throughout the duration of her life, when
Jesus appeared to Faustina, he would take different forms. Sometimes
he came as a little child who played on the chapel floor. Sometimes he

appeared bloody and beaten as in his Passion. Other times he wore a crown of thorns, and at others robed in a bright tunic surrounded by glorious light. Each time his appearance reflected a desire from the heart of Jesus. As a child, he invited Faustina to greater trust, as a child with a parent. When in his Passion, he wished for Faustina to console him. When in his glory, he desired for Faustina to worship him.

This particular evening, Jesus was clothed in a white garment that flowed from his neck to his ankles. Light emanated from Jesus, and his glorified wounds were visible. He remained still before her, but he had one foot slightly ahead of the other in a posture of walking forward toward her. His right hand, the biblical symbol of power, was raised in blessing, while his left hand gently pulled aside the garment at his breast. Beneath his garment, his heart was revealed and from it, much like the blood and water that flowed from his pierced side, emanated two rays of light, one red and one pale. The face of Jesus reflected serenity and peace as well as power and eternity. He is God, fully powerful and omnipotent, and fully man, coming in love to his children. He appeared to be joyful while intent and earnest, as if he wished to communicate something. His gaze was cast downward, as if he looked down from the Cross.

Faustina gazed unspeaking upon this vision in wonder and joy. She only faintly grasped at the time the power of this revelation and the importance of the moment. After a time, Jesus spoke to Faustina and made several requests of her. First, Jesus wanted a painting made of him as he appeared in this moment. It would be a painting made with a real brush, to be seen and venerated by the Church. Across the bottom of the painting were the words Jesus, *I Trust in You!*

His second request was that the finished painting be venerated in the chapel of Faustina's convent and eventually throughout the whole world. It was to be hung where all could see it and be officially recognized by the Church, and he promised great blessings to those who would venerate the image.

Jesus also asked that the first Sunday after Easter be observed as a day of mercy. The Church was to glorify the mercy of God on this day. Priests were to proclaim God's mercy from the pulpits across the world.

Later on, Jesus taught Faustina a prayer which used the rosary beads called the Divine Mercy Chaplet. Again, he promised many graces to those who would venerate the painted image and pray the chaplet. It was Jesus' desire that the faithful pray this chaplet often, especially for sinners and the dying.

The trials that followed this first appearance left Faustina with great doubts of the authenticity of her experience. Some of her sisters ridiculed her, labeling her as a hysteric and a fanatic. Perhaps they were right. . . . At first, even Faustina's confessor told her it was all symbolic, that Jesus wanted her to paint the image on her soul, but not on canvas. Her Mother Superior would do nothing without a concrete sign from God. Doubts plagued Faustina's mind and heart. Was this a true vision or some figment of her imagination? She asked this question of God explicitly.

Along with her own doubts, real obstacles rose in Faustina's way as she sought to fulfill Jesus' requests. She gives no indication in her writings that she strategized a plan of action. She was probably mostly unaware of the large undertaking this was to be. First, she would have to find a good painter to create the artwork, and this in itself would require funding. Second, a priest would need to believe her and take up her case before the local bishop. This bishop would then have to bring it to the nuncio, who would need to bring it before the pope. If all this were to happen, the pope himself would have to publicly proclaim the new feast day for the whole Church. These steps sound straightforward, but in reality each are a lengthy and extremely difficult process.

Jesus promised Faustina support through a priest she had yet to meet. His name was Fr. Michael Sopocko. This priest was to be Jesus' faithful servant who would help carry out the task assigned to Faustina. But this brought only more questions to Faustina's mind and heart. Who was this priest? Where was he and when would he come to Faustina's aid? Again, Faustina's only response was to wait in hope and trust.

TUESDAY OF THE FOURTH WEEK OF LENT

FR. MICHAEL SOPOCKO, GOD'S FAITHFUL SERVANT

Therefore, He had to be made like His brethren in all things, so that He might become a merciful and faithful high priest in things pertaining to God, to make propitiation for the sins of the people.
HEBREWS 2:17

Readings from the **Diary**: *597, 609, 675, 1014, 1256*

Today we must turn our attention to priest who aided Faustina in her work of promoting Divine Mercy. Fr Michael Sopocko was a strong support and guide to Faustina during her years of suffering. His holiness and wisdom were officially recognized by the Church at his beatification in 2008. If little has been written about Faustina, even less so has been written about Fr. Sopocko. Bishop Henryk Ciereszko writes in a biography about Fr. Michael:

> *The history of the efforts to have the Divine Mercy message and devotion approved and accepted by the Church and the world cannot be credited to anyone else but Blessed Michael Sopocko. Most of the enormous amount of apostolic work this extraordinary man has done for God's revelations seems to have been hidden from*

74

*the public and somehow the only the person publicized in
relation to this salvific event is Sister Faustina.*[20]

Fr. Sopocko, Priest of Mercy

Fr. Sopocko was a priest of mercy, who epitomized what the Catholic
priesthood should be. He was a very talented man who excelled
at every ministry in which he served. He gave brilliant university
lectures, yet he could just as quickly roll up his sleeves and build small
village schools for the poor or hustle through the trenches of war as
a military chaplain.

Fr. Sopocko was born in 1888 to a noble family in the Vilnius
region. Though from a noble lineage, his family was poor, yet
strongly patriotic. Recognizing his talents for learning, his parents
sacrificed much to send him to Catholic school. He entered
the seminary at the age of twenty-two. Normally, study for the
priesthood is a six-to-ten-year process. However, Fr Sopocko's
process was cut short. In 1914, World War I was abruptly
unleashed. Due to the rapid militarization of Europe, any young
man of military age risked being conscripted, even if they were
seminarians. The seminary formators were concerned and decided
to advance multiple candidates to the priesthood. Whoever was
deemed prepared enough in the essentials of the priesthood would
be ordained. Fr Sopocko writes:

> *In spring 1914, during my exam sessions one evening I
> was summoned to the rector's office, he said I was to join
> the group of seminarians on retreat, and then I was to be
> ordained a sub-deacon. I was astounded by the decision,
> as I had not expected that for some time yet. I did not
> even know how to pray using a breviary. I did not feel I*

---

20 Bishop Henryk Ciereszko, *Endless Mercy* (Dublin: Divine Mercy Publications,
2013), 6.

was ready to be ordained, but the rector and my confessor,
Fr Michnowicz, persuaded me to do so.[21]

Fr. Sopocko's first duty as a priest was the spiritual care of the
Polish soldiers. He was assigned to a small parish near Vilnius, where
he quickly became active in the war effort. These trenches were where
he cut his teeth as a priest. The violence of war and the bloodletting
that raged around Fr. Sopocko, and those entrusted to his care, made
him very sensitive to the need for mercy in the world. Both world wars
spanned the prime years of his life and left a mark upon his soul that
shaped his priesthood.

Even while serving in the trenches, Fr. Sopocko helped keep the
schools in the area alive. The poverty that the war created made any
type of schooling difficult to come by. On numerous occasions Fr.
Sopocko involved himself directly in the running of the schools. This
work in pedagogy served him well, as he was named a spiritual guide
and confessor in the seminary after the end of World War I.

Fr. Sopocko served as the spiritual father of the seminary for five
years. The figure of "spiritual father" is an important role in the seminary.
It refers to a priest who has no authority or interaction with the seminary
formation team, but rather lives with the seminarians, guides them
through spiritual direction, and helps them as needed in their studies and
ministries. In short, he is a role model present among the seminarians. Fr.
Sopocko was valued by the young men entrusted to him and was a highly
praised spiritual director. Little by little, Fr. Sopocko's intellectual vigor
became apparent, and he became the History of Philosophy professor as
well as the assistant professor of Theology.

Fr. Sopocko lived each of his roles to the best of his capacity. He
was a pastor, not just an administrator; an educator, not just a professor.
He lived his priesthood as a true vocation and not a job.

---

21 Taken from Fr Sopocko's "Priest Formation in the Spiritual Seminary" in Bishop
Henryk Ciereszko, *Endless Mercy* (Dublin: Divine Mercy Publications, 2013), 26.

WEDNESDAY OF THE FOURTH WEEK OF LENT

FR. SOPOCKO AND FAUSTINA MEET

Mercy is a very ancient Latin word and, during its long history in those who have experienced it, has acquired delicate meanings from the many nuances of language of the two terms that make it up: "misery" and "heart". . . . In Greek, the language of the New Testament, the word for mercy is eleos—*a word that is familiar to us thanks to the prayer* Kyrie eleison, *the invocation of the Lord's mercy. This is turn is a translation of the Hebrew word* hésèd, *one of the most beautiful biblical words, that stresses the faithfulness of God's mercy for each man.*[22]

Readings from the **Diary: *34, 54, 61, 578***

In addition to his work in the seminary as a professor and spiritual father to the seminarians, Fr. Sopocko also had a few side ministries that kept him very busy. One, which he maintained throughout his life, was acting as confessor and chaplain to different communities of religious women. Many of these convents had no official chaplain and relied upon any priest who could come for the sacraments. Due to the extent of experience and his brilliant mind, requests for retreats and spiritual guidance from these religious communities flooded Fr. Sopocko's desk.

It was in this capacity that Fr. Sopocko came to Faustina's convent.

---

22 *Mercy in the Fathers of the Church,* Pastoral Council for the Promotion of the New Evangelization, 14.

On June 1, 1933, Faustina had confession with Fr. Sopocko for the first time. This encounter between a humble nun and an active and busy priest of mercy took place two years after Jesus revealed his message of Divine Mercy to Faustina. It was one of those events unnoticed by the world's eyes, yet it marked a decisive moment for the Church and the message of Divine Mercy.

For years, Faustina had yearned for a stable spiritual guide, someone who could help her navigate her encounters with Jesus (see *Diary*, 34). Her prayer and experiences were leading her down pathways she had never imagined, and for two confusing years, she had carried the message of Divine Mercy mostly alone. Thankfully, Faustina received some consolation in two visions she received in which she saw Fr. Michael Sopocko praying in a chapel (see *Diary*, 54, 61). She knew this priest was to be her guide. It seems, however, that Fr Michael was not so aware of this at first. He came to hear confessions, unaware that his life and mission were about to change. His duties as confessor were never much out of the ordinary. A religious community of women who were very busy at work was such a homogenous group that the time hearing confessions was also somewhat repetitive. But this day would be different!

When Faustina entered the chapel, she immediately recognized Fr. Sopocko from her visions. She knelt in the confessional, unsure of where to start. This was the priest promised her, but the fear of being rejected yet again must have been present. Would this priest believe her?

For Fr. Sopocko, the confession itself was extraordinary and hard to believe. First, Faustina presented herself as a visionary, in the fullest sense of the word. This alone is enough to make any confessor skeptical. It is not uncommon for priests to be approached by people claiming to be visionaries or who are experiencing extraordinary phenomenon. A great many of these people tend to be somewhat unbalanced, and their claims require no follow-up. It is common practice in the Church that private revelations are to be first ignored in order to see if they persist. If they continue, they are tested. Only rarely will these private revelations be given any sort of credence by the Church. Thus, most priests do not believe initially any such claims from a penitent. Faustina also claimed she had seen Fr. Sopocko in a previous vision and that he was to listen to her and fulfill the plans which Jesus had communicated.23

As these things were hard to believe, the authenticity of both the message and the messenger needed to be tested. With this knowledge, Fr. Sopocko at first acted accordingly. He listened to her kindly and asked questions, inviting her to pray more. His advice was to be cautious, to be prepared to suffer, and to be patient (see *Diary*, 270). Faustina noticed the hesitation in Fr. Sopocko, and this caused her to be more reserved than she had originally planned (see *Diary*, 144). Faustina had to reveal a vision that was not just informational but imperative. It contained a mission, something she had to do—and something she had to convince Fr. Sopocko that *he* had to do.

As soon as Faustina left the confessional, Fr. Sopocko went to find the Mother Superior of the house. He discreetly asked what type of religious sister Faustina was. His hope was that learning how Faustina lived her religious life would shed light on the situation before him. Mother Superior told him that she was a model religious, balanced and simple. To rule out some type of unhealthy mental state, Fr. Sopocko requested that she be evaluated psychologically.

When Faustina passed the psychology tests with flying colors and he was sure this was not just a fantastically weaved story, Fr. Sopocko then tested Faustina spiritually. If this woman was truly an instrument of God, then her holiness or progression in the spiritual life should be apparent. He began having regular dialogues with Faustina, focusing on her prayer, virtue, and growth in holiness. He encouraged her that if this was indeed the work of God, the message of Divine Mercy should first be formed in her soul. This, he insisted, was the focus of God's work.

---

23 Faustina hesitated to reveal everything to Fr. Sopocko at once. Rather, she shared small parts of her Divine Mercy experience each week during her confession. This occurred over the summer of 1933.

THURSDAY OF THE FOURTH WEEK OF LENT

THE WRITING OF THE *DIARY*

*He [Christ] runs to you, because he already hears you when you reflect inside
yourself, in the secret of your heart. . . . He embraces you to raise those who
lay on the ground, and to ensure that he who was oppressed by the weight
of sins and bent towards earthly things, again raises his eyes to the heavens,
where to search for his creator. Christ embraces you, because he wants to
remove the weight of slavery from your neck, and set a sweet yoke on you.*
ST. AMBROSE[24]

Readings from the Diary: *90, 1765, 1766*

Since Fr. Sopocko was a busy man and could not come to visit Faustina
as often as she would have liked, he made a decision for which the
whole Church owes him a debt of gratitude. He asked Faustina to begin
keeping a diary to record her experiences. When Fr. Sopocko would
visit her, he would read through the diary, occasionally taking it with
him for a time. In this way he could study the messages and pray over
them in his free time. Her writings would eventually fill six notebooks.
At one point, Faustina burned what she had written.[25] She then rewrote
what was burned, but in a summary fashion. And thus, the *Diary* today
is in part a reconstruction of what she originally wrote.

Faustina wrote in her diary during her spare time, quite a feat for

---

24 *Exposition of the Gospel of Luke*, 7.229–230.
25 See *Diary,* footnote 42.

a busy religious sister whose duties in the kitchen and garden filled the hours when she wasn't in prayer or with her community. Her community itself proved to be another obstacle to her writing. The buildings in which Faustina lived were very small, creating a cramped existence among the sisters. Very few areas provided a private setting. As a result, Faustina did not always have a quiet spot in which to pray or write, but she wrote wherever and whenever she could. This meant that keeping her diary a secret was a tall task. At times, sisters would approach and asked questions, prompting Faustina to hurriedly close the notebook and smear the drying ink. This was a constant frustration to Faustina. Over time, her sisters wanted to know why Faustina was writing so much.

Because Faustina never gave a direct answer regarding her work but continued to try and hide her activities, many of her sisters began to resent her apparent oddities. This resentment was compounded by the fact that Fr. Sopocko would spend long hours talking with Faustina whenever he visited. This resentment became a daily trial for Faustina, and there were few moments in which she received any respite. Even something as simple as waiting for confession had its thorns; no one wanted to wait in the confession line behind Faustina as she might talk to Fr. Sopocko for an extended period of time. Faustina would often choose to go last so as not to bother any of the sisters.

The resentment directed toward Faustina was not limited to the Second Choir sisters with whom she interacted the most. The First Choir sisters also noticed the attention Faustina received from Fr. Sopocko. This special treatment, as well the extra writing and praying, did not seem proper for a Second Choir member, whose duties were menial and supportive in nature. Faustina's pursuit of these higher activities seemed to take away from her ordinary duties at the time and as an infringement upon the status quo of the convent structure.

Ewa Czaczkowska writes:

The task of writing her Diary was not an easy one for Sr. Faustina. First of all, she was not well educated; she had only finished less than three grades of elementary school. Second she didn't have circumstances conducive to writing. She was busy with work in the garden, and in her free moments, she had to conceal her writing from the other sisters. Faustina wrote on a nightstand, on her bed, and in some convents, like Vilnius, she wrote on a small table, separated from the other nuns by a screen. She was always on the watch, so that she could close and hide her notebook at any moment. In such moments, she stopped mid-sentence, and did not return to finish her thought.

Sister Borgia Tichy, Superior of the Vilnius house from December 1934 onwards, wrote,

She devoted her free time to writing her diary entries, which she hid scrupulously. This is what roused the sisters more than once to make many more or less spiteful comments, particularly because this was connected with more frequent contact with the confessor during the week. That is why she received the nickname among the sisters of 'kasztelanka' her ladyship.[26]

---

26 Ewa Czaczkowska, *Faustina: The Mystic and Her Message*, 229.

FRIDAY OF THE FOURTH WEEK OF LENT

THE TWO APOSTLES OF DIVINE MERCY

Why did not God send the promised Savior at once? Here too we must discern the infinite Mercy of God. God delayed the fulfillment of His promise, that men might come to know the full misery of sin, that they might understand the need, the necessity of Redemption, that they might long for Redemption, and thus prize all the more that vast Mercy that was revealed in it. If a man heedlessly squanders his patrimony, and then at once regains it, he will not realize the evil of his spendthrift way: he can only learn it by the suffering that wastefulness has brought on him. Thus men, after long centuries of woe, understood the horror of sin, and began to cry out: "Drop down dew, ye heavens, from above, and let the clouds rain the Just: let the earth be opened, and bud forth a Savior, and let justice spring up together" (Isaiah 45:8).

BL. MICHAEL SOPOCKO[31]

Readings from the **Diary:** *90, 1513, 1687*

Despite these trials and difficulties, Fr. Sopocko maintained his arrangement with Faustina until her death. She would write in her diary, and he would read and review what she wrote. When time allowed, he would visit, and she would open her heart to him. They also wrote to each other, filling in the gaps for when Fr. Sopocko could not make it to the convent. Faustina was the original Apostle of Divine Mercy; Fr. Sopocko the answer to her prayers. Faustina was the sacrificial offering, like incense cast on the fire that burned out quickly. Fr. Sopocko was a slowly burning candle, providing and spreading the light wherever he went. They both followed the path of Jesus, the crucified one. Jesus called himself the "crucified Master" (*Diary*, 1513). And "a disciple is not above the teacher, but everyone who is fully qualified will be like the teacher" (Luke 6:40).

Once Fr. Sopocko was convinced of the authenticity of Faustina's claims, his mission was to bring the revelations of Divine Mercy to the Church. His goal was twofold: to commission the image of Divine Mercy that would be venerated throughout the whole world, and to convince the Church, namely the bishops and the Holy Father in Rome, to establish the second Sunday after Easter as the Feast of Divine Mercy.

Fr. Sopocko understood that to obtain approval for the feast day, a strong theological case for its existence would need to be prepared. What he needed was to take Faustina, her visions, and her diary out of the equation and garner the evidence that was already present in Scripture and Tradition. Bishops would be more likely to support sound theological arguments than arguments made from a personal diary.

The work of developing the theology of Divine Mercy needed time, and as we have seen, Fr. Sopocko was a very busy priest. Between his personal life to building schools to forming seminarians to his teaching, preaching, and writing, how could he give up one of his ministries to dedicate time to this new endeavor? This was not an easy decision, but Fr. Sopocko was convinced that God was at work through Faustina. This extra cross on his shoulders and the need to pray much over Divine Mercy was a sure sign that God was at work.

Above all, Fr. Sopocko's mission was to suffer and to be faithful. In this sense, the frustrations and apostolic roadblocks he encountered were allowed by God to aid him on his path to holiness.

Herein lies the key to Fr. Sopocko's success in spreading the message of Divine Mercy: he was a man faithful to God's will. He did not dream of personal accomplishments or accolades in the eyes of the world. He was not afraid of the cross as long as it was God's will. And as soon as he recognized Divine Mercy as God's will for him, he did not simply study it as an outsider would; instead, he embraced it in his life. He accomplished something that is much easier said than done: to accept Divine Mercy in his life and believe that he was loved. He wrote about Divine Mercy from the experience of his own prayer and his own heart to the point that the diary of Faustina became secondary.

SATURDAY OF THE FOURTH WEEK OF LENT

THE PAINTING OF DIVINE MERCY

Those who sincerely say 'Jesus, I trust in You' will find comfort in all their anxieties and fears. There is nothing more man needs than Divine Mercy—that love which is benevolent, which is compassionate, which raises man above his weakness to the infinite heights to the holiness of God.
St. John Paul II, Poland, June 7, 1997

Readings from the **Diary**: *177, 1520, 1521*

Fr. Sopocko had an important role in commissioning the image of Divine Mercy. The very first image that was painted was done by an artist with whom Fr. Sopocko lived, a painter named Eugene Kazimirowski. Once hired, it took him six months to finish the painting. During that time, Faustina visited him once a week to oversee the work and give instructions on the finer details of the image. Faustina herself was never fully satisfied with the portrayal of Jesus, complaining in her diary that the artist could not capture the same magnificence as the Jesus of her visions.

Once the painting was completed, Fr. Sopocko sought permission from the local bishop to have it displayed publicly in his parish. At the time, Fr. Sopocko was trying to keep Faustina out of the public eye, and so he had a difficult time explaining the portrait and its significance when seeking the permission. Faustina pressed him gently that the picture be hung quickly in accordance with the urgency that Jesus communicated to her, but Fr. Sopocko proceeded with caution. Obtaining the local bishop's permission was more complicated than Faustina realized and would have a lasting impact on how the faithful viewed Divine Mercy. For the first months of the painting's existence, it hung in Fr. Sopocko's apartment.

In November 1934, Fr. Sopocko took the painting with him to his new assignment as rector of St. Michael's Church in Vilnius. While Fr. Sopocko did not hang the painting for public display, he did put it up in a private corridor within the church used mostly by the parish sisters.

The moment for displaying the image came when Fr. Sopocko was asked to preach on a Second Sunday of Easter. Fr. Sopocko casually requested that the image of Divine Mercy be temporarily placed beside the pulpit to aid his preaching. This "temporary" nature meant that there was no need to ask the bishop for permission. It wasn't until April 4, 1937, that Fr. Sopocko received permission from the archbishop to officially hang the image in his church. This was a full six years after Faustina received the request from Jesus.

FIFTH SUNDAY OF LENT

THE WINDOW WOUNDS OF JESUS

Let us fall into the hands of the Lord,
but not into the hands of mortals;
for equal to his majesty is his mercy,
and equal to his name are his works.
SIRACH 2:18

Readings from the **Diary:** *60, 1447, 1121*

The revelation of Divine Mercy to Faustina was the beginning of a beautiful gift from God to his Church and the world. Only a few days after her first vision of Divine Mercy, Faustina saw an image of Divine Mercy that included God the Father (*Diary*, 60). This is what she saw: God the Father, surrounded in radiance, looked at the world from heaven. Directly between God the Father and his view of humanity was the image of Jesus stretched out on the cross. Jesus was positioned in such a way that when the Father wanted to look at his creation, he had to do so through the pierced hands of Jesus.

From this image, Faustina understood that God the Father gazes upon the world in the context of the loving sacrifice of His Son, epitomized by his wounds. This window wound of love is the lens through which God the Father sees everything. Jesus stands in the gap, raising his hands and shielding the Father's sight from the sin of mankind. Jesus' wounds are the ultimate filter of love and mercy.

Through her diary, Faustina invites us also to delve more deeply into what Divine Mercy means for us personally. First, this image reveals not only the mercy of Jesus, but of God the Father. Jesus is the Father's gift of mercy to the world, and he continually grants his mercy to us because of the love he has for his Son.

Thus, even though our sins are many, they are *always* seen through the saving wounds of Jesus. The arms of Jesus never grow tired. He is a faithful and merciful high priest, continually interceding for us until the end of time. The look of the Father is always and eternally a look of mercy. God the Father enters into the world and gives his grace to us through the action of his Son. With this understanding of the gaze of the Father *through* the Son, the Eucharist takes on a deeper meaning as well. As we gaze upon the host in adoration, God the Father gazes back upon us through the host.

In response, an apostle of Divine Mercy must learn to look at the world through the wounds of Jesus. In this way, darkness becomes light, lost souls become saved, and what is sinful becomes sanctifiable. No problem is too hard; no mountain is too high. The wounds of Jesus keep us from being angry and judgmental, since every person has been saved by the blood of Jesus and is a sharer in the love of God.

MONDAY OF THE FIFTH WEEK OF LENT

CHRIST WITH A TRULY HUMAN HEART

For judgment will be without mercy to anyone who has
shown no mercy; mercy triumphs over judgment.
JAMES 2:13

Readings from the **Diary:** *1537, 50, 177, 1074, 1190*

At the core of Divine Mercy is the open heart of Jesus. In the image revealed to Faustina, Jesus' left hand is pulling back his tunic to allow the love of his heart, in the form of the two rays, to burst forth into the world. Not only does the love of Jesus pour out upon us, but we are invited inside to learn what we can about this divine heart. In addition to the image of Divine Mercy, the diary of Faustina describes other encounters that hint at the enormous reality of Christ's human and divine heart.

When we speak of the heart of Christ, we must tread lightly. Centuries of brilliant minds and ardent hearts have searched the pages of Scripture to better understand the Sacred Heart of Jesus. The recent development of the psychological sciences and today's penchant for plumbing the depths of the human experience have lent themselves to the use of theology, and this meeting of faith and reason has given us new insight into the person Christ.

We can only begin to understand the person of Christ when we acknowledge the unity between his humanity and his divinity. As a human, he had human emotions. As God, they were perfectly ordered. That, as God, Jesus chose to embrace his emotions is telling. As a society we tend to frown at emotions. Often an emotional person is considered a weak person. Yet this is not so. Our wide range of emotions that daily come and go are part and parcel of the human experience. Emotions are reactions to life revealing that a person is fully alive. Even so, emotions should enrich our lives, not control them. *Jesus, as man, was enriched by his emotions.*

Every human heart is a mystery that we long to unravel. Yet in the words of Blaise Pascal, "The heart has its reasons, which reason does not know."[27]

That Jesus was a man deeply in touch with the world and with his own heart is evident throughout the Gospels. He was not passive before the events of his life but acted and reacted to what he experienced. Consider the following moments in the life of Jesus: he wept over Jerusalem. He wept for Lazarus. He rejoiced in the Spirit. He blessed and embraced little children. He walked prayerfully through the fields, thirsted by a well, and he became angry and drove the moneychangers from the temple. He was friends with men and women alike. He grew tired and slept in a boat. He loved and obeyed his mother. He suffered a deep sorrow in Gethsemane. He sweat blood before his Passion yet remained steadfast to his Father's will.

Jesus, the Son of God, descended to Earth to become one of us. He did not display a godlike immutability or indifference. He did not remain aloof to our existence. He fully lived our human experience and loved and blessed us even more. No part of our humanity is too small in his sight, not even our emotions.

---

27 Blaise Pascal, *Pensées* (London: The Penguin Group, 1966).

TUESDAY OF THE FIFTH WEEK OF LENT

THE FLAMES OF MERCY FROM THE HEART OF CHRIST

The more the human conscience succumbs to secularization, loses its sense of the very meaning of the word "mercy," moves away from God and distances itself from the mystery of mercy, the more the Church has the right and the duty to appeal to the God of mercy "with loud cries."

DIVES IN MISERICORDIA, 15

Readings from the **Diary:** *71, 229, 1728*

In one section of the diary, Jesus described the emotions of his heart as "flames of Mercy." These flames of mercy burn within his heart, clamoring to be spent. The heart of Jesus contains a deep longing for the salvation of souls, and the love of his heart is so great that when someone rejects his love, his own heart makes him suffer.

Love is something that by its very nature must be given away, and in the giving we offer a part of ourselves. A gift of love that is not responded to returns to the giver as pain. Unrequited love is one of the deepest human experiences, one that can make or break a person. Jesus yearns for a response to his love, and in Faustina's story, he yearned for all of her love.

By delving into the heart of Jesus, we discover his "holy jealousy." Jesus wants our attention and our love, and he waits for the moment we turn our gaze to him. One of Faustina's many duties was to decorate the chapel with flowers. She wrote that once she saw some beautiful flowers and, without much thought, decided to bring them to the room of a sick sister. As she walked to the sister's room, she passed by the chapel. Jesus stood at the chapel door and gently asked her who the flowers were for. What a subtle question that revealed an even more subtle distinction in Faustina's heart! While she was going to do a good thing, she had forgotten the best thing. Jesus knows the tiniest beat of our hearts, and he listens attentively, hoping that we will be as attentive to him as he is to us.

This perfect divine love that fills the heart of Jesus goes out to every person, yet often mankind spurns the offer. To be despised and spurned by others is a painful experience, and Jesus must endure not only rejection, but also the weakness of those specifically dedicated to him, his very ministers. Every Christian is called to be an apostle of mercy, but his priests and consecrated souls should be so par excellence. Rejection from a stranger hurts, but the pain is easily forgotten. Rejection from a friend or a loved one burns. This is the pain of betrayal.

Priests often do not display Jesus' own mercy, never preach about his mercy, or simply do not even understand it. Perhaps these ministers began their work with generosity, but little by little the experiences of rejection and indifference have taken their toll. They close their hearts off from their flock so as to not suffer. To stop caring is to numb their hearts by protecting them and building a wall around them. A priest who simply becomes an administrator of his parish rather than a spiritual father perhaps should not be so harshly blamed. Jesus himself revealed the suffering it caused him to drink his chalice. The agony in the garden was not an invention by the evangelists for dramatic effect. It was real. And as a real mystery of Christ, Jesus shares that mystery with souls who are willing.

WEDNESDAY OF THE FIFTH WEEK OF LENT

THE HIGHEST MOUNTAIN IN
THE SPIRITUAL LIFE

*We usually recognize a writer or speaker by his style. A concise style
expresses the serene mind of Plato, the profound thought of Aristotle, the
noble soul of Cornielle, the religious detachment from the world of St.
Augustine, and so on. The Prophets, too, have their own style. To begin
with, they tremble, hesitate, lament; then gradually they enkindle, stir
to life; next they thunder, flash forth lightnings, let inspiration have its
way with them; then at last they cease. . . . Our Lord's style is wholly
different; its distinctive feature is simplicity and unction. The simplicity
characterizes the wisdom of God; the unction, His Mercy. There is no style
simpler, and at the same time more sublime, than that used by Christ.*

BL. MICHAEL SOPOCKO, 222

Readings from the **Diary***: 1717, 1728*

Let us leave aside the life of St. Faustina and Fr. Sopocko for the
moment and reflect upon Divine Mercy in our own souls. How does
one become an apostle of mercy in one's daily life? It is commonly said
that you cannot give what you do not have. Therefore, the first step
in becoming an apostle of Divine Mercy is to accept Divine Mercy in
your own life.

In order to fully embrace the mercy of God, we must first live with a proper understanding of the life of grace. If we set out on the Christian journey with a faulty understanding of grace and virtue, we risk hindering ourselves on the way. We may be able to formulate three possible mindsets that people adopt as they set out on their spiritual journey. Let us examine each in turn.

The first mindset is *sin-centered*. The vision of God that this approach fosters is a vision of God as Supreme Judge. He sets down a body of rules that must be followed. He judges us according to these rules and is always "on the lookout" for sinners. His divine wrath must be appeased by doing penance. God deals with us sinners only begrudgingly, the Cross of Jesus being something our sins forced him to do. The motor of this spiritual life is fear. Since our life is inevitably sinful, we must do all we can to avoid the pains of hell. Because of this, much emphasis is placed on performing penances, expiatory prayer, strict rigidness in liturgy and prayer, much focus on praying for the suffering souls in purgatory and a general disdain for the world. Jesus' Second Coming is seen as the moment where God will definitively clean house and punish sinners.

This approach to the spiritual life, while having within it plenty of important elements of the faith, when it is exaggerated too far, has an insidious affect inside the Church and is more common than people tend to think. I use the term *insidious* quite intentionally. By definition, it is a very gradual and subtle evil that over time causes harmful effects. Usually the damage is seen only too late. If the devil's goal in the past was in the Garden of Eden to get Adam and Eve not to trust God as a Father, this sin-centered approach to Christianity continues this diabolical trend today.

This spiritual view creates overly scrupulous souls. They spend their waking hours making sure they haven't sinned; they see each situation in life as an occasion of potential sin, and they see God as a judge up in the clouds who angrily is looking down on them, expecting them to fall. To avoid sin and atone for their failures, they focus on many pious devotions and prayers and have an unhealthy desire to read and hear anything regarding apocalyptic end times. All these external prayer and devotions can appear to reveal a person of deep spiritual life, but their motive is not love; it is fear. Sadly, this is not holiness.

The second mindset is *virtue-centered*. This is certainly a much better approach than the previous. However, in its rather exaggerated form, its shortcomings also produce an insidious affect. Here the spiritual life is presented as a series of challenges. There are an infinite number of hurdles that a person must jump over. Growing in holiness is trying harder, always climbing higher, always fighting longer. The saints are perceived as men and women who fought bravely and endured heavy penances and long fasts. They become in our collective mind so lofty and divine that they are no longer realistic goals. Nevertheless, we treat them as such, presenting them as models of the way. This vision of the spiritual life uses a line from the book of Job: "The life of man upon earth is a warfare, and his days are like the days of a hireling" (Job 7:1, Douay-Rheims 1899).

This mindset emphasizes that we must win the battle, and our salvation depends mostly on our own effort. While the previous approach sees God as a Judge whom we fear, this approach sees God as a King whom we serve. Here the Christian life is confused with the virtuous life. The two are not opposed, but they are not exactly the same. The Greeks, before Christianity had arrived on the world scene, had already discovered in their philosophy the nature and definition of the cardinal virtues. They had a well-developed moral code to go along with them. But a virtuous life is not the same as a grace-filled life. When Christ became incarnate in the world, it was not so we would all try to become virtuous people who are polite and who go to Mass on Sunday. This would be an outrageous reductionism! Yet we fall into it often.

The insidious effects of this approach are seen in the fruits, not the process. First, it is self-centered. The virtues are ways of perfecting our human nature, and so little by little a pride develops regarding our spiritual exercises. We are looking mostly in a mirror instead of looking to Christ.

Second, at times the hard work of growth in virtue leaves a person looking very often for a reward, be it material blessings in this life or spiritual blessings in the life to come. The thought process is that if we are faithful and try hard, God will bless us. The focus can become very narrow, looking for the blessings of God but not the God of blessings. A good job, strong financial security, peace in life, healthy children, and blissful marriages are all looked upon as rewards and blessings from God. But what happens when these "blessings" do not come? Life actually more often can give us sickness and hardships. These are always a part of life. When life no longer makes sense, the virtue-centered approach fails to provide answers.

With the virtue approach, a lot of effort is expended in the beginning, and it helps people to achieve a certain stability in their spiritual life. They form habits of prayer and virtue. But at a certain point they are blocked from advancing further. They get to the top of a mountain and then run out of mountain to climb. The attraction to a virtuous life for its own sake is not enough of a motor to overcome life's greatest challenges. This is spiritual burnout. While this virtue-driven spiritual life has its benefits, it does not highlight enough God's grace or his action in our life. The spiritual life, before it is arduous, is actually very gentle. Overall, the virtue-centered approach can be a good starting point, but it is too limited in scope for a truly Christian way of life.

The third approach is *love-centered*. The hardest part of the spiritual life is not the climb up the mountain of virtues away from the desert of sin. The hardest part is accepting the mercy of God in your life and truly believing you are loved. At first blush this may seem incorrect because most Christians would say that they believe in God's love and His mercy. But for this truth to sink down to the depths of our soul and not be merely a cheap affirmation on our lips, one that we say we believe but do not really act like it, requires a lifetime.

It is a usual starting point in a person's first steps toward union with God that a focus on sin is necessary. We must let go of sin and uproot vice from our lives. This process may begin out of fear of divine punishment, but at some point it must begin to be done out of love for God.

The void that has been created by the removal of vice must be replaced by virtue. For this reason, the acquisition of virtues will be a focus for a time. But again, virtue is acquired ultimately because it makes one more Christlike, not simply because it makes one more humanly perfect.

Growth in holiness should produce a soul that is alike to those that Jesus told us would be able to enter heaven: the childlike (Matthew 18:3). On the heights of holiness we do not find the rigid ascetic who has beaten himself into submission to many penitential rules, but we find men and women whose union with Christ has given them a certain spiritual freedom as beloved children of God.

> *As we progress in the spiritual life, the cause of God is not served by more rules but by fewer. The instinct of love, a balanced instinct now, takes over for the multiplicity of rules of the earlier stages, and does this work better. We do not mean a desertion of the ascetical life, never that, but a more relaxed and childlike attitude toward the will of the Holy Spirit.*[28]

The temptation to look on God primarily as a judge or a king is very strong. A better approach would be more "catholic" (i.e., universal, whole, complete). It is to understand God as Judge, King, and Father all at the same time, with the primacy on God's Fatherhood.

---

28 Fr. Dominic M. Hoffman, OP, *The Life Within: The Prayer of Union*, 72.

THURSDAY OF THE FIFTH WEEK OF LENT

A KEY TO ACCEPTING DIVINE MERCY

But for that very reason I received mercy, so that in me, as the foremost,
Jesus Christ might display the utmost patience, making me an example
to those who would come to believe in him for eternal life.

1 TIMOTHY 1:16

Readings from the Diary: *1121, 1142, 1361, 1541*

How do you view God? If you tend to see him as only as an angry Judge,
then this is the God you will present to people. If God is only a King who
must be obeyed, then this is the image of God that you will show others
through your actions. However, you should reveal no other image of God
than that revealed by Jesus. God is Abba, Father. God is love. The source
of our joy is that God revealed himself as love and mercy itself.

The false spiritualities that we reviewed yesterday can create
spiritual wounds in our souls over time. The healing of these wounds
is a slow process that takes time and grace, both of which the Church
has in abundance.

The Catholic Church has many founts of grace that we can drink
from in order to soothe our spiritual hurts. One of the most powerful
sources is the Eucharist. The Eucharist is Jesus' self-expression of his love
as self-donation. Frequent reception of Holy Communion brings Jesus
himself into our souls and enables us to accept his personal love and

mercy. Alongside frequent Communion is the practice of Eucharistic adoration.

Adoration is the quiet revolution of the Church, and this revolution is twofold. It is the revolution of time, that which has kept the Church grounded and true, century after century, Christ's constant presence with us. It is also the transformative revolution of real people having real encounters with their God. Many eras of human history begin with some sort of revolution—for example, the Industrial Revolution or the French Revolution. Yet the most important of all is the Eucharistic Revolution where God meets his people day after day, hour after hour.

Jesus longs for us to lean back and rest our weary heads and heart upon his chest. Adoration chapels are places of prayer, peace, and quiet, where people can gaze upon the Beloved and in return are gazed upon by Him. It is a living out of the Song of Songs. The Beloved peers into the room through the monstrance upon the altar.

> *Behold he standeth behind our wall, looking through the windows, looking through the lattices.* (Song of Songs 2:9)

And Christ and the contemplative soul repeat to each other:

> *How beautiful you are, my love, how very beautiful! Your eyes are doves behind your veil.* (Song of Songs 4:1)

It is here, upon the altar, that one can find the Heart of Jesus revealed sacramentally. The type of prayer that happens in these chapels is primarily a restful prayer of simply being before God as we are. There are no loud hymns being sung, and despite the occasional litany, Rosary, or chaplet, the place is silent. And in the silence the Lord comes, speaking in a whisper and in a heartbeat. This is the modern-day trysting place of every heart today.

The man or woman who has been constantly told as they grew up that they were not good enough, not beautiful enough, that they were a sinful problem, have assimilated these lies deep into their subconscious. Even though they may intellectually know it is a falsehood, until the lie is uprooted from the depths of their soul, its insidious effect will remain. These lies are the bane of Christian life. Like a hidden and stealthy poison, they do their damage little by little without us being even aware that it is happening before it is too late.

During adoration a person spends some amount of time, typically an hour, praying before Jesus in the Eucharist. It is here that grace can penetrate deeply in our souls, even without us being aware of it. Here, sin and vice are uprooted, the poison of the lies we believe are drawn out, the strength of forgiveness is granted, and the imperfections are refined. Allowing Jesus this time is one of the greatest means we have to become an apostle of Divine Mercy.

FRIDAY OF THE FIFTH WEEK OF LENT

※

THE SACRAMENT OF DIVINE MERCY

Our Lord instituted this Sacrament out of His love for God and His Mercy towards men. The love of God is revealed in it, for through the Eucharist men come to know better the wisdom, power, goodness and Mercy of God, who gives us not only His graces, but Himself, to remain always with us. Here, too, is shown the love of God for the Church, which is entrusted with His true Body, preserves It, feeds on It, and unceasingly offers It to the Father, and love for each member of His Bride, the Church, for He desires to be the food of each. The Eucharist is especially an act of Christ's love, as Man, for all those who believe in Him; it is the crown of all His acts and works, like some vast solar system, in which love moves all things, and radiates out to the ends of time.
BL. MICHAEL SOPOCKO, 209

Readings from the **Diary***: 1804, 1810, 1811*

Perhaps one of the most iconic stories about the power of adoration comes to us from the Cure of Ars, St. John Vianney. St. John Vianney struggled with a vice-ridden village in France where there was very little spiritual pursuit. He understood that the foundation of all spiritual change begins with the Eucharist, and so he began promoting Eucharistic devotion within his parish. This was in part the catalyst of the revolution of that little village of Ars. As Eucharistic life took off in his parish, St. John noticed an old farmer who would come every day and just sit in the church for hours.

> *Contemplation is a gaze of faith, fixed on Jesus. "I look at him and he looks at me": this is what a certain peasant of Ars in the time of his holy curé used to say while praying before the tabernacle. This focus on Jesus is a renunciation of self. His gaze purifies our heart; the light of the countenance of Jesus illumines the eyes of our heart and teaches us to see everything in the light of his truth and his compassion for all men. (CCC, 2715)*

How powerful is one's gaze! In adoration, the Lord Jesus looks deep into our soul, and we open our soul to his piercing gaze. It is an exchange of gazes, because just as we open our souls to the gaze of Christ, he opens his Sacred Heart to our gaze, and this interchange of love is what heals us. It is here, under the gaze of Christ, that we are able to recognize our worth in the eyes of Jesus and that the bitter wounds of loneliness, inadequacy, and lack of faith in the goodness of God are healed. The very fruit of adoration and Eucharistic Communion is a greater acceptance of mercy and a deeper humility to embrace it. Thus, for a Christian who has experienced Divine Mercy, adoration is not an option; it is essential.

The time one spends in prayer is irrelevant as well. What is only a few minutes can have the effect of hours, and vice versa. What seems like much time often is no more than a few minutes. What seems like a short prayer can have lasted hours. In adoration the laws of time seem to be suspended. Time touches Eternity, heaven comes to earth, and Love opens a window into the human soul.

St. Faustina spent countless hours in adoration. Her full religious name was Maria Faustina of the Most Blessed Sacrament. She spent many mystical moments in prayer before the Eucharist and at Mass.

Her diary reveals a woman who tried to enter into the chapel at every free moment. Occasionally, she would see the image of Divine Mercy in the monstrance as two rays of pouring forth from the Host, just as in the image. It was in these moments that she discovered that the Eucharist was none other than the Sacrament of Divine Mercy. What the image portrays, the sacrament does. These rays of grace and mercy touch each soul who, in faith, comes before the Blessed Sacrament.

SATURDAY OF THE FIFTH WEEK OF LENT

_____

EUCHARISTIC CHILDHOOD

*Because the L*ORD *your God is a merciful God, he will*
neither abandon you nor destroy you; he will not forget the
covenant with your ancestors that he swore to them.
DEUTERONOMY 4:31

Readings from the **Diary:** *593, 1021, 1074, 1075*

If we were to examine the lives of the saints and make a list of all their common virtues, simplicity of soul would be listed over and over. In general, the saints are uncomplicated people who filled their hearts with trust, hope, and a reverent wonder at God and things divine. Simplicity in the practice of the spiritual life is often referred to as spiritual childhood. St. Faustina is not the chief exponent of this virtue—that place belongs undeniably to St. Thérèse of Lisieux, who brought to us her "little way." However, Jesus made the necessity of this virtue clear to Faustina and provided her with some beautiful explanations as to what it means to be spiritually childlike. Thérèse developed and wrote about her "little way" from the point of view of the child looking to her father. Jesus, through Faustina's *Diary*, reveals the beauty of simplicity from the viewpoint of the Father looking down on his child.

Before delving much further into this topic, let's turn to this virtue's original source, the Gospel. In chapter eight of the Gospel of Matthew, Jesus is teaching his disciples a lesson through a child:

> *At that time the disciples came to Jesus and asked, "Who is the greatest in the kingdom of heaven?" He called a child, whom he put among them, and said, "Truly I tell you, unless you change and become like children, you will never enter the kingdom of heaven. Whoever becomes humble like this child is the greatest in the kingdom of heaven.* (Matthew 8:1–4)

We know that Jesus traveled on foot throughout the Holy Land. He crisscrossed the map during his three years of public ministry. Around him, and sometimes jockeying for the best places near him, were his apostles and disciples. Alongside the apostles was a hidden group of women, mentioned specifically in Luke's Gospel. This small group of women followed behind the group and seems to have ministered to Jesus and his roving band of apostles.

While the men were concerned at times about themselves, about who was the greatest, who was the closest to Jesus, the women seemed to have focused not on themselves but on Jesus. We know that they provided for Jesus out of their material talents. Thus, the women's purpose was more hidden but more essential; they focused on the one thing necessary: taking care of Jesus. Only afterward was there some thought as to what they would receive from Jesus. Hidden in the pages of this Scripture is the constant theme in the spiritual life of the need to be focused and centered on Christ alone. If we take our eyes off of Christ and look to ourselves, we fall.

This must have been a familiar scene for Jesus and his apostles. They are walking again between villages, speaking among one another, occasionally asking Jesus questions, while farther back on the road, the women followed. At some point Jesus notices tension growing in his small group of apostles. We don't know how this dispute arose, but perhaps the twelve men had formed some type of pecking order. Maybe they put value in the order in which they were called; maybe it had something to do with the professions of their past lives. Whatever the case, Jesus knew their hearts and knew that they needed a change in perspective.

Jesus slows down to let the women catch up. We can assume that with the women there might have been a few children as well, and as the women approach the apostles, Jesus sees the one he is looking for. With the utmost respect, Jesus takes a toddler from one of the women and lifts the child into his arms. He then walks into the midst of the apostles and places the child on the ground next to him. Perhaps the child, happy to be with Jesus, becomes shy before the apostles and so clings to Jesus' tunic.

The apostles' need to be recognized by Jesus revealed their desire for the esteem and praise their positions could bring. The child wanted to be near Jesus simply for who Jesus was, not what Jesus could do for the child. Jesus invites his apostles to be just like this little child, clinging to Jesus and nothing else.

This simple child becomes for us an icon of the spiritual life. To be perfect is to be as a little child. In one swoop, Jesus shatters our false notions of power and ascendancy, flipping modernity's view of greatness on its head.

Three characteristics are particular to children. First, they are willing to be led anywhere. Second, they are willing to be taught truth and believe mystery. Third, they have not lost the capacity of wonder. Therefore, we can say that in a way, *in the spiritual life we grow into children*. Adults are autonomous, independent, and go their own way. A child is so dependent on its parents that it cannot survive without them. This should be little by little how the spiritual life crystallizes itself in a soul: the person realizes each day that they need God more than ever.

Faustina had these three characteristics. She was willing to be led by the hand of Jesus away from the dance floor of the world and into the darkness that was her religious life. She believed in his words and trusted in Divine Mercy, even when his words and teachings were mysterious and unbelievable to some. Faustina marveled at God's work and action, glorifying and adoring him for his great mercy. In his book *The Name of God Is Mercy*, Pope Francis decries what he calls the "degradation of awe." Children have the capacity to wonder, to be amazed and in awe of the world and creation. The simplest things can bring a child to rejoice and clap their hands in delight. As adults, we lose this ability to be in awe. When we do so, the wonder and beauty of salvation itself, that we have been so loved by God that he died for us personally and the gates of heaven are open, can be lost and no longer move our hearts. Believing and trusting in mercy maintains the wonder and amazement before the love of God. It is something we never get used to, but it sparks something new in our lives each and every day.

PALM SUNDAY

THE SUFFERING JESUS

On this occasion we encounter two mysteries: the mystery of human suffering and the mystery of Divine Mercy. At first sight these two mysteries seem to be opposed to one another. But when we study them more deeply in the light of faith, we find that they are placed in reciprocal harmony through the mystery of the Cross of Christ. . . . Dear friends who are sick, who are marked by suffering in body or soul, you are most closely united to the Cross of Christ, and at the same time, you are the most eloquent witnesses of God's mercy. Through you and through your suffering, he bows down toward humanity with love. You who say in silence: "Jesus, I trust in you" teach us that there is no faith more profound, no hope more alive and no love more ardent than the faith, hope and love of a person who in the midst of suffering places himself securely in God's hands.

PEPE BENEDICT XVI[29]

Readings from the Diary: *642, 532, 533*

Today Jesus enters liturgically into Jerusalem. Longstanding Christian tradition recognizes the event of Jesus' entry into Jerusalem as the opening of the mysteries of Holy Week. It is a mystery of entry,[30] and as we walk into our parish churches with palm fronds, we ourselves

29 Pope Benedict XVI, Shrine of Divine Mercy in Krakow-Lagiewniki, May 27, 2006.
30 Gregory Collins, OSB, *Meeting Christ in His Mysteries: A Benedictine Vision of the Spiritual Life* (Collegeville, MN: Liturgical Press, 2011), 171.

enter mystically into the Passion of Our Lord. Jesus enjoys the shouts of the little children in this moment, but he also knows the adult voices around him will shortly be shouting "Crucify him!" For this, he suffers.

The pages of Faustina's diary are sprinkled with appearances of a suffering Jesus. Over time she became no stranger to the thorns, the wounds, the scourging, and the weight of the Cross. This in and of itself is a strong message of mercy for us to unpack today. Even the image of Divine Mercy includes a wounded yet glorious Jesus. If we understand the Passion as Jesus' ultimate gift of love, the greatest triumph of Divine Mercy in time, then it is fitting that the very image we identify with Divine Mercy should appear as such. Theologically, Jesus suffered only once historically in time. He is not suffering "historically" today; rather, we refer to his mystical Passion.

So, what are the image of Divine Mercy and the appearances of the suffering Christ to Faustina trying to teach us? The diary of Faustina is in line with a long tradition of the Church that speaks of a mystical suffering in Jesus. This suffering isn't another Passion, but the same suffering of the Passion mystically re-presented. God is outside of time. This is a difficult concept for us time-bound creatures to grasp. We think in terms of before, during and after, but for God, things simply are. This re-presentation of the Passion is the historical suffering of Jesus experienced in the eternal present of heaven. In a sense, we can say that for Jesus, his Passion then is also his Passion now.

More important than seeking to understand this mystical suffering of Jesus is asking ourselves what it means for us. If Jesus suffers, what is the repercussion in my life and living of my faith? That Jesus would even reveal his suffering to us is a request of some sort, a revelation that requires a response. But what? Somehow we are at the threshold of a great mystery. The words of St. Paul to the Colossians will be for us a biblical starting point. They are revealing as much as concealing this mystery:

Now I rejoice in my sufferings for your sake, and in my
flesh I complete what is lacking in Christ's afflictions for the
sake of his body, that is, the church. (Colossians 1:24)

In May 1926, a few weeks after Faustina took her religious habit, Pope Pius XI published this Church teaching. He wrote:

Now if, because of our sins also which were as yet in
the future, but were foreseen, the soul of Christ became
sorrowful unto death, it cannot be doubted that then,
too, already He derived somewhat of solace from our
reparation, which was likewise foreseen, when "there
appeared to Him an angel from heaven" (Luke xxii, 43),
in order that His Heart, oppressed with weariness and
anguish, might find consolation. And so even now, in a
wondrous yet true manner, we can and ought to console
that Most Sacred Heart which is continually wounded by
the sins of thankless men.[31]

This is the doctrine of consoling the heart of Jesus. The response to the suffering of Jesus is for every one of us to become that nameless, faceless angel in the Garden of Gethsemane that the Father sent to strengthen and console his Son. We are truly able to console the suffering heart of Jesus historically and mystically, both then and now. Our efforts to love and console Jesus in our daily lives are known to God, who is and was and will always be omniscient. Because of the omniscience of God, we can say with utmost confidence that the sacrifices of all peoples everywhere in time are truly present to Jesus in his physical Passion.

---

31 Pope Pius XI, *Miserentissimus Redemptor*, https://www.vatican.va/content/pius-xi/en/encyclicals/documents/hf_p-xi_enc_19280508_miserentissimus-redemptor.html.

The mystical suffering of Jesus also envelops the sins that occur all over the world presently. In addition to consoling the heart of Jesus, the knowledge of Jesus' suffering is an invitation to reparation and atonement for the sins of our culture. It is an invitation to enter into this present darkness and bring his mercy and love, first to ourselves and then to those around us. When we learn to pray not for what we need, but for what Jesus desires, we will have passed a milestone in the spiritual life.

HOLY MONDAY

THE CHILD JESUS AND FAUSTINA

Suffer the little children to come unto me, and forbid
them not; for of such is the kingdom of God.
MARK 10:14

Readings from the **Diary:** *80, 184 529, 562, 575, 1481*

Jesus first revealed himself to the world as a little child at Christmas. He could have simply appeared in the world as an adult. He could have hidden his birth and all his human weakness and only revealed himself when he was ready, but he didn't. He chose to be born, opting for the eyes of all the world to see him as a baby. He sent his angels to gather the shepherds and the star to guide the magi. The shepherds represented the people of Israel, and the magi represented the Gentiles, so, symbolically, the whole world was in attendance at Jesus' birth. This fact shouldn't be overlooked.

St. Faustina had many extraordinary graces during her lifetime. Paging through her *Diary*, one is quick to notice a pattern: when Jesus appears to her in the context of the Mass or during Eucharistic adoration, he appears most often in the form of a child.

Often during the Sacred Liturgy, Faustina would watch a playful child Jesus as he held the priest's vestments. Sometimes the child Jesus would play at the feet of the priest, sometimes at the altar, and sometimes he would walk up to Faustina in the pew all with the spontaneity and playfulness of a child. The child Jesus would often disappear at the moment of the breaking of the bread. Faustina understood that Jesus didn't simply disappear, but was now present in the Eucharist, blessed and broken on the altar. It was the presence of the child she didn't always understand, and so once she asked Jesus why he chose to come to her so often as a child. Jesus gave her an answer on two occasions (see *Diary*, 184, 1481). It was to teach Faustina to be simple.

These conversations with the Child Jesus appear only after the revelations to Faustina of Divine Mercy. With this in mind, the revelation of childlike simplicity should be understood in the context of this new phase in her life. Jesus comes as love and desires that we receive him in love with the love of a child.

Without this lens of love and mercy, the Gospels seem to be full of folly. Over and over, Scripture presents to us the paradoxical nature of Christian living: dying gives life, losing is finding, forsaking all is gaining all. What reason deems illogical, love understands. Christ himself, fully human and fully divine, is a mystery that will forever surpass our human understanding. It is no wonder, then, that Faustina presents to us another paradox when she calls Jesus the "Divine Prisoner of Love" (*Diary*, 80).

God cannot be contained or controlled by anything. He has no limitations, no weakness, and no finitude. To call God a prisoner seems impossible. Yet Jesus willingly made himself limited, weak, and vulnerable out of love for us. By taking on human flesh, Jesus became one with his creation. By taking on a human heart, he accepted experiencing the pains of love. In the Eucharist Jesus humbled himself to be at the mercy of his ministers. Jesus has chosen to need us, to need our love. This is love beyond anything we can ever imagine. This revelation is the single greatest good news that the world has ever known. This message is placed upon the shoulders of each and every apostle of divine mercy.

HOLY TUESDAY

THE CHILD JESUS AND US

At that time the disciples came to Jesus, saying, "Who is the greatest in the kingdom of heaven?" And calling to him a child, he put him in the midst of them, and said, "Truly, I say to you, unless you turn and become like children, you will never enter the kingdom of heaven. Whoever humbles himself like this child, he is the greatest in the kingdom of heaven. Whoever receives one such child in my name receives me."

MATTHEW 18:1–5

Readings from the Diary: *783, 25, 683*

Jesus wishes to keep company with us as a child. How awesome to think that that Creator of the Universe desires to be near us! The God who commands armies of angels comes to us in littleness so as not to frighten us. He wants to be so close to us that he can carry us close to his heart.

The link between the Child Jesus and the Eucharist is rich in meaning. The manger in which Jesus was laid was a place for food. Christ's presence in the manger symbolically announces that Christ has come as Divine Food, as the Bread of Life. We are to partake of the supper of the Lord. Hence every altar in the Catholic Church symbolizes both Calvary and Bethlehem (*Bethlehem* means "House of Bread"). The manger is our altar, and the bread of life is found there. All are called to partake.

The Eucharist is a mystery to approach with faith and simplicity. Those who accept this mystery in their lives without complicating it with skepticism find a warm and comforting presence.

For an apostle of Divine Mercy, the Eucharist should have pride of place. Faustina was in the habit of making a little room in her heart where she would always accompany him. This secret inner place in her soul was accessible to only Jesus. When we allow the Lord of Mercy to enter into our heart and take up residence, the understanding of the mysteries of mercy follow. But how do we allow Jesus this space in our hearts?

Welcoming Jesus into our hearts at the time of Communion is key. Jesus lamented to Faustina two things when it comes to reception of the Eucharist: 1) many people are not prepared to receive Communion and 2) when they receive Communion anyway, they never think of him at all. He told Faustina that this is like a second Passion for him (see *Diary*, 1598).

As for all things, we should turn to our spiritual mother, Mary, for the perfect way to welcome Jesus into our hearts. Mary received the very first Communion when she carried Jesus in her womb. Her body created that first dwelling place, the first secret inner sanctum. How hard it must have been for her to let go of that intimacy when the time for her to give birth came and she had to place him in the manger for all the world to see. Some came to adore, others to scoff, some even to blaspheme. At the end of his earthly life, Mary had to leave his body in a tomb. But she never let that space within grow cold. She filled it, reflecting upon all things in her heart, so that when the apostles began to celebrate the breaking of the bread as Jesus had commanded, she was ready and waiting to receive the gift of her son once again. Tradition holds that for the rest of Mary's earthly life, she devoutly received the Eucharist, giving us all an example to follow.

This Holy Week, Mary is a good model for us to follow as we accompany Our Lord. Mary appears to Faustina before moments of particular suffering. It seems that Mary knew that the suffering in Faustina's life would be hard, and she could not help but encourage Faustina to embrace the crosses. She invited Faustina never to defend herself from a pierced heart.

In one moment, Faustina saw the Blessed Mother in Heaven with a sword piercing her heart. Mary is standing before all of humanity, interceding for us and shielding us from the wrath of God (see *Diary*, 683).

The tender and motherly heart of Mary could not resist coming to Faustina before moments of great suffering. As she did for Jesus, being near him in his Passion, so Mary does for any soul that flies to her protection. Her role as Mother of Sorrows is clear: to help us not to run from the Cross of Jesus but to embrace and accept it.

HOLY WEDNESDAY

THE PETITIONS OF JESUS

On the last day of the feast, the great day, Jesus stood up and proclaimed,
"If any one thirst, let him come to me and drink. He who believes in me, as
the scripture has said, 'Out of his heart shall flow rivers of living water.'"
JOHN 7:37–38

Readings from the **Diary:** *1617, 1160, 1224, 1485, 1540, 715*

Throughout the *Diary*, Jesus makes many small requests of Faustina that can also be applied to ourselves. Some of these are so simple that we could easily overlook them, but incorporating these small customs into our daily routine can lead to intimacy with God that perhaps we never knew existed.

The first petition of Jesus is to be thanked. There are four basic types of prayer: Adoration, Contrition, Thanksgiving, and Supplication. Supplication is commonly divided into two more categories: Intercession and Petition. All of these types of prayer are valid and beautiful and have a place in our prayer life, yet some come more naturally than others. When a child is young, one of the first things they learn is to ask questions and request favors, yet harder to learn is gratitude for what is received. We need more an attitude of thanksgiving in prayer than an attitude of petition. God is not a vending machine that we insert the coin of petition into, get what we asked for, and forget about until our next need. God wants us to ask things of him. He wants to be a providing and loving Father. Our prayers of petition please him but returning and thanking him for his gifts please him even more. The danger is to let petition become all the prayer we ever make. Gratitude, gratitude, gratitude!

The other danger with our petitions is that when we ask God for things, we usually present God with our own solutions. We aren't presenting a problem so much as presenting a solution. And this solution often involves our human desires and plans, not necessarily the plans of God. We want our problems solved our way and not God's way. It is a tough challenge to bring our needs to Jesus and let him solve them as he wishes, when he wishes, and then to thank him for whatever he does. Difficult, yes, but the fruit it will bear in our spiritual life will be tremendous.

The next petition Jesus has for us is to accept and act upon his divine graces immediately. Sometimes an inspiration comes to us, and if it doesn't match our own ideas, we push it aside. We all like to shop around for the things we want, but there is not à la carte Christianity where we can take what we like and leave the rest behind. God and religion are not products to consume. There is a danger to this attitude. It induces us little by little to reject the things we don't like, any cross we don't wish to carry, and do only that which is easy and agreeable.

Throughout the *Diary*, the phrase *to glorify mercy* is frequently used by Jesus. In this phrase we find the final petition of Jesus that we will reflect on together. He wanted Faustina and the whole Church to glorify his mercy. The wonders of his mercy needed to be made known to the whole Church, not just through the feast of Divine Mercy, but also through the actions of every apostle of mercy. Thanking Jesus for his mercy and glorifying it in our lives means living our Christian faith with joy and sharing it with anyone we meet. Our faith cannot be a private matter that we keep hidden from the world. A privatized form of Christianity that overlooks both our neighbor and the mystical body of Christ is a false Christianity.

There are many people who work for Jesus and undertake many large projects, but if they do it for their own glory and not for Jesus' glory, their efforts are misguided. This is a subtle form of spiritual pride that can find its way into even very pious souls. They heap upon themselves great sacrifices apparently for God, but only follow their own personal whims. It is not for love of God but love of self. Each apostle of mercy needs to be simple and childlike in their work for the Kingdom. This does not mean never doing projects and initiatives but rather keeping in mind who we are working for and who is ultimately bringing about success. A spiritual child knows that all good fruits come from God and that our actions, separated from God, mean nothing.

HOLY THURSDAY

A CRUCIFIED LOVE

Now there was leaning on Jesus' bosom one of
his disciples, whom Jesus loved.
JOHN 13:23

Readings from the **Diary:** *1002, 1053, 1702*

Jesus granted Faustina a foreknowledge of the sufferings to come in her life. This was a cross freely offered to and freely embraced by Faustina. Suffering is the inevitable lot of mankind. The Christian, however, transforms the daily struggles of life from unbearable burdens into meaningfully redemptive crosses. The grace and purpose Faustina drew from the Cross became the source and foundation which sustained her, as well as introduced her to the merciful heart of Jesus.

In Christian marriage, it is said that the two become one flesh, one heart. It is then the life work of the spouses to grow in love and understanding of each other to the point that the needs and desires of one are intimately understood by the other. This is the goal of the spiritual life as well and is why we say that marriage is a foreshadowing of what heaven is like. Imagine now how attentive to her spouse is a bride of Christ, who through spiritual marriage by her vows are called here on earth to an interchange of hearts with Christ. Every Christian is called to drink the chalice of the Bridegroom in heaven, but there are those here on earth who have the ability to feel the heart of Jesus, to sense his needs and desires, to love the world with this heart and who dedicate their lives to console his Sacred Heart.

This heart-knowledge comes only through prayer, not study. It is a grace similar to the one St. John, the Beloved Disciple, received when he rested his head on the Heart of Jesus. St. John the Apostle is perhaps the first to understand the Heart of Jesus after his mother, Mary. He walked the path of the Bridegroom, drank from this chalice, rested his head on his heart, and stood fearlessly at the foot of the Cross.

It is interesting to note that special preference is given to St. John in the life and writings of Faustina. In fact, it is only the Gospel of St. John that is referenced in the pages of her diary. Jesus even once asked Faustina to make her spiritual readings and retreats solely from its pages. Let us turn to this Beloved Disciple for a moment to understand what made him so different from the other apostles.

On the night before his Passion, the Gospels tell us that Jesus shared a meal with his apostles. Over the course of three years, Jesus had eaten many meals with them, but none as ceremonial and central to his life as the Last Supper. It was the Passover meal, and the solemnity of the occasion was matched by the solemn composure of Jesus.

We can imagine how the scene may have unfolded. The apostles and Jesus recline around a low table, with their left arms supporting themselves and their right arms free to eat the meal and pass the food. Of the order of seating, we know only that John sat beside Jesus, so close in fact that he could lean back and rest his head upon Jesus' chest. We can assume the proximity of two others close to Jesus: Peter and Judas. Peter we may understand, as he is the Prince of the Apostle, the chosen "rock." But Judas? The Gospels tell us he was close enough to dip his bread in the same bowl as Jesus, but perhaps there was another reason for his closeness. Knowing what we know of the heart of Jesus, perhaps he had Judas nearby in order to continue to try to convert his heart. Jesus knows his betrayer; he knows that the heart of Judas has become cold. The money bag tied at his waste jingled each time Judas moved and symbolized the great wall that had come between disciple and Master. Jesus gave Judas every opportunity to repent, to avoid this disaster, to always be his friend. The last words that Jesus spoke to Judas were a petition for friendship: "And Jesus said to him: Friend, whereto art thou come? Then they came up, and laid hands on Jesus, and held him" (Matthew 26:50).

At the meal, Jesus announced that one of the Twelve will betray him. What a stir this must have caused! And what an interesting reaction from the apostles. It seems that rather than accusing each other and pointing fingers, they grew quiet, each one asking, "Surely it is not I?" As each apostle questioned his own integrity, Peter signaled to John to find out who Jesus meant. John is also burdened with sorrow, but it is a sorrow that mirrors the anguish in the heart of Christ. John leans back upon the bosom of Christ, *in sinu Jesu.* "Master, who is it?" His question probes; his action consoles.

At John's request, Jesus motions toward Judas, and hands him a morsel of food. It is an odd exchange, one that the rest of the apostles do not clearly understand. Judas wordlessly departs into the night, and they think only that he has gone somewhere to purchase something for the feast.

John saw and heard the whole exchange from his privileged position. There on the heart of Jesus, he discovered the strength, tenderness, and mercy of God. John listened to the priestly prayer of Jesus, and later watched as each and every word uttered found fulfillment. John drew strength from the divine heartbeat, a strength none of the other apostles would possess that night. John's anguish brought him closer to Christ, and Christ became his strength.

GOOD FRIDAY

⁓⟨⟩⁓

SHARING THE CROSS WITH JESUS

*Then Jesus told his disciples, "If any want to become my followers,
let them deny themselves and take up their cross and follow me.*
Matthew 16:24

Readings from the **Diary:** *446, 604, 648, 1059, 1061, 1580*

Christianity is a religion of mysteries. The creed of the Catholic Church
contains a long list of truths so unfathomable that perhaps we can say
one will never fully comprehend their depth and breadth. The Son as
eternally begotten of the Father is one such truth. Before these mysteries
we are all invited, like Moses, to respectfully take off our sandals. Our
celebration of the Sacred Mysteries is an attempt of the human soul
to reach out and touch these Divine Truths, knowing we will never
fully grasp them. This effort is not in vain; we can know something
about them, just not everything. This is why a Christian mystery is
not an impossible enigma. It is accessible to us in part through our
participation in divine life.

God is a mystery, as are his will and his nature. The fully divine
and fully human life of Christ is another mystery. The deeper into
the faith you go, the longer this list of mysteries seems to become:
the Virgin Mary, the Virgin Birth, the Immaculate Conception, the
Church founded on the apostles, the Eucharist, the sacraments, etc. At

the center of all these mysteries lies the heart of Christianity: the Pascal Mystery, the Passion, Death, and Resurrection of Jesus.

Every Catholic dies and rises with Christ in Baptism. It is through this sacrament that we are sealed with the sign of our salvation, the Cross. The Cross is not something we will ever fully understand or ever assimilate in this life. Thus, the Cross will be a lifelong love affair for us. Its weight on our shoulders changes—at times weighing heavily in our lives, while at other times it seems to weigh no more than a feather and we walk with the wind at our backs. Some Christians run from the Cross, yet in doing so they only make new crosses for themselves. The Cross is here to stay because God's love is here to stay.

It sounds strange to say, especially within many a contemporary Christian church, that St. Faustina was "blessed" with a life of crosses. In her fifth notebook, written toward the end of her life, she reflected over her short life. She noted that her life on Earth paralleled the life of Jesus (see *Diary*, 1580).

This ability to focus on the Beloved and walk with him wherever he leads is a fruit of spiritual grace. The human heart does not naturally want to suffer and walk up Mt. Calvary. In fact, if Jesus had not walked up Calvary first, it would be wrong for us to seek to do so. For a Christian, we follow the Lord wherever he leads us and only where he leads us. Yet because he has led the way for us, the forgotten mountains of suffering have become privileged places for Christians of all time.

Faustina was once blessed with a vision of Jesus on the Cross (see *Diary*, 446). After contemplating him for a time, she then saw all the souls of the world. Each soul was linked to a cross, their own cross. Some were like Jesus, crucified as he was. Other were not crucified but were holding their crosses firmly in their hands. Another group was not holding their crosses or nailed to them, but unhappily dragging them behind them. These are the words of Jesus that completed the vision:

Do you see these souls? Those who are like Me in the pain and contempt they suffer will be like Me also in glory. And those who resemble Me less in pain and contempt will also bear less resemblance to Me in glory. (Diary, 446)

Another time, Faustina was granted a vision of Fr. Sopocko (see *Diary*, 604). She saw him, as well as his soul. In the midst of his work and the heavy burden placed on him as he sought to spread the message of Divine Mercy, he was suffering very much. Yet Faustina learned that Fr. Sopocko's sufferings were to become a crown in heaven.

The Cross of Jesus was a way of life for Faustina. She realized little by little that she had to die in order to bear fruit. This willingness to die with and for Jesus is the heart of an apostle of Divine Mercy. Without it, we do not truly grasp the deeper meanings of all Jesus is asking of us. He wants friendship and union with each soul, and this is the privileged path of the Cross here on Earth. You cannot be an apostle of Divine Mercy without finding your personal place in the Passion of Jesus.

HOLY SATURDAY

PRAYER IN THE *DIARY*

Our Lord accepted the repentance of Dismas (the good thief), and, with great love and Mercy, gave the magnanimous reply: "Amen I say to thee, this day thou shalt be with me in paradise" (Luke 23:43). Here Our Lord not only promised, but gave him, with complete certainty, more than he had asked. For Dismas had begged the Saviour for no more than to remember him at some unspecified time: and now he learnt that on that very day he was to be in the happiness of Heaven. . . . What a happy hour of death—an hour of death that we all may envy—after so many years of evil-doing and crimes! O how great and unfathomable, how infinite and immeasurable, the Mercy of God that flowed into the soul of the thief at the last moment of his life on earth, permitting him, so to speak, to steal Heaven.
BL. MICHAEL SOPOCKO, 112

Readings from the **Diary**: *739, 275, 1427, 201, 65, 279, 348, 825*

Today we wait in silence outside the tomb of Jesus. The Church today dwells in hushed tones and silences. Today is a day for silent prayer. In the *Diary*, there are so many examples of prayer to draw from that we will only look at a handful. Here, in no specific order, are some of the best gems about prayer that can be mined from Faustina's *Diary*.

Prayer as Profound Silence

The language God often uses to communicate his deepest love for a soul is the language of silence. Anyone who wishes to communicate with him must learn this language. The words of God are so infinite and majestic that no human words can ever express them; thus silence is the way of God. God is Love; therefore, he communicates essentially by love, not words. Prayer is more a moment of receiving love as opposed to a transmission of information. The idea of prayer as a phone call to heaven in which one speaks and informs is inadequate. Prayer is an embrace between Earth and Heaven. This is a transmission of love that does not need words. Faustina longed often for moments of silent prayer. She said many vocal prayers as part of her community life, but throughout her diary what Faustina truly pined for was time alone with Jesus. She frequently requested permission from her superiors for extra times of prayer, either late at night or early in the morning. She needed this deep breath of prayer in order to live her mission as apostle of Divine Mercy.

When we liken prayer to deep silence, we are not saying that our prayer should not contain words or that oral prayer has no place or purpose, but that our prayer should contain love above all. The deep love expressed between God and the one who prays is transmitted through subtle movements of the heart and surpasses human understanding. When Faustina was in the novitiate, she experienced a long, dry darkness in her prayer and religious life. She could not feel the presence of God nor hear his voice speaking to her in her soul. This experience can lead one to abandon prayer; however, Faustina endured, focusing on God and not on her own feelings. She began to go to the Eucharist to speak "with profound silence," a prayer from heart to heart. This example is perhaps the *Diary*'s best image of prayer: seeking out the Beloved in the Eucharist and there communing with God in silence.

Prayer as Gentle Loving

One day Faustina was in a moment of prayer. She had just received Communion at Mass and stayed in the chapel afterward for some time to pray for all the people for whom she had intentions. This prayer of petition is possibly the most common form of prayer people know and use. As Faustina prayed, it seems she offered a very intense pleading before Jesus, and as Jesus listened and received this display of fervor, he approached her gently and chided her for exerting herself with so many words.

Jesus wished to transmit to Faustina that she didn't have to "convince" him to do something with her prayers. He loved those on her list more than she did and already wished to help them. A frantic pleading before God as if he were a judge to sway or a king to convince means we aren't approaching him as a Father. Jesus wished Faustina to gently trust in him. Our prayer is not to be complex, frantic, or overly nuanced; it is to be simple, a loving glance turned toward heaven.

Prayer as Hidden

Jesus loves hidden souls (see *Diary*, 275). Throughout the *Diary*, Faustina refers over twenty times to God as "Hidden God" and to Jesus as "My Hidden Jesus." She even wrote a poem with each line starting with "Hidden Jesus" (*Diary*, 1427). One truth that any Christian seriously pursuing a life of prayer learns is that our relationship with God is more hidden to the world than visible (see *Diary*, 201). Even if we have a public ministry or active apostolate, who we are before the eyes of God is always the same. We always possess a personal treasure in God that can't be shared or expressed completely in words to a fellow human being.

As we have mentioned, Jesus preferred to commune with Faustina in a hidden way. She herself was very careful to guard her life with Jesus from the eyes of her sisters and the world. As her prayer life progressed, she desired more and more to disappear from the eyes of the world. Some days she wrote that she could live in uninterrupted prayer with

Christ even in the midst of her busy day. She always hid her diary from others, and despite all the miraculous occurrences in her life, she never spoke of them to anyone but her confessor. Faustina harbored a secret treasure all through her life.

We can only speculate at why Jesus desires to be so hidden as it doesn't always make sense to us. In John's Gospel we see Jesus hide his arrival to Jerusalem: "After his brothers had gone to the festival, then he also went, not publicly but as it were in secret" (John 7:10). And he specifically preferred our prayer to be secret: "Whenever you pray, go into your room and shut the door and pray to your Father who is in secret; and your Father who sees in secret will reward you" (Matthew 6:6).

One reason for this secrecy could be that the love between the soul and Christ is so intimate that, if exposed to the world, it would be like throwing pearls before swine. Prayer takes place in the depths of the soul, and it is only by turning inward in prayer that the soul achieves that which it desires. Prayer must lead us inward to the very center of our soul where God alone dwells.

Keeping our life with Jesus hidden helps avoid the pitfalls of spiritual pride and spiritual vanity. The path to holiness is paved with many stepping-stones. The very act of overcoming our desire to show off our spiritual life as a trophy for all the world to see and envy is a spiritual milestone in and of itself. In the beginning of the spiritual journey, we often can't help but share with everyone our most recent prayer experience. As time goes by and we grow and mature, it is quietness and reservation that leads to greater spiritual depth.

Through hidden prayer our souls learn to enjoy being seen by God alone. It is only before God that we are truly ourselves with no mask and no baggage. This truth of who we are before God reaches the very marrow of our soul with such a delight that it spurs us to seek even more time alone with the Beloved.

Christ desires our times of prayer more than we do! At the risk of sounding cliché, it is said that misery loves company. This human experience of desiring support from a loved one in a time of crisis seems to also be an experience that Jesus, who is fully human, experiences. His Passion was not a historical moment that came and went. In this "mystical passion" of Jesus, each Christian can enter into the mystery and participate in it. This possibility is reflected by Jesus' plea to his apostles to watch with him for an hour, and in the *Diary* it is reflected in his desire that Faustina relive with him his Passion. Jesus wanted Faustina, his mystical spouse, to participate in his mystical life. This grace is to allow Jesus to relive his mysteries in us, from the Incarnation to his Resurrection and everything in between.

In her diary, Faustina makes a wildly audacious claim: God cannot be happy without her (see *Diary*, 1120). In this sense, each soul is a part of God's creation of love, into which he poured painstaking detail. We are each the "object of His special action" (*Diary*, 824). We are unrepeatable beings that come forth from the heart of God, and his heart can only be filled when each one of us returns to that place. Forever, in my soul, there is the mark of the divine Creator. This Creator desires that I return this to him by glorifying him. Faustina sees her life itself as God's masterpiece, the Divine Artist taking painstaking care of the image he creates (see *Diary*, 825).

EASTER SUNDAY

A KAIROS OF MERCY

For the Lord your God is gracious and merciful,
and will not turn away his face from you, if you return to him.
2 Chronicles 30:9

Readings from the **Diary**: *1067, 1019, 1020*

The light of Easter morning has dawned, and with it the apostles and disciples are faced with an amazing and confusing fact: the tomb is now empty! Wonder, confusion, awe, and a thrilling sense of new life are emotions that are setting their hearts on fire.

The empty tomb of Easter morning sheds light on the type of Church that Jesus intended to found. Jesus has conquered death and sin. Forever more, all those who wish may receive mercy. The task of the Church today is to continue making this invitation to receive mercy. Our Church must be always on the lookout for the lost sheep. The Church is a place for lost sheep, for sinners. Every man is a sinner, but not every man will acknowledge this. The Church is a home for everyone. Additionally, the Church is a place of rejoicing when each lost sheep is found. This is a task that brings joy and is done in this light. We are not weary apostles trudging through the world in darkness, frightened and joyless. We have hope and we have Christ—we have all we need!

The Church is to be like God the Father, always going out to find the lost children, always willing to become dirty by going out into the streets, always seeking what is lost until the end of time. Pope Francis calls the time of the Church today a *Kairos*. This is a period of time with religious significance, a holy time, a time of grace. And thus, the message of Divine Mercy, as in the Year of Mercy, is a Kairos for the Church. All things are to be made new. The Church is most alive and truly herself when she leads humanity to the font of mercy.

The apostle of mercy is a person who believes in God's love, encounters this God of love in prayer and the Eucharist, and daily shoulders the Cross of Jesus with love. When an apostle of mercy goes out into the world to share the love of God, they do so with a detachment from self and their own plans. They go on behalf of God as his joyful messenger. What we do for God should always be what God does through us.

We are not the protagonists in the work of evangelization. It is better to think of our work as being participants in evangelization. We are the children of the King, and as such, we go about his affairs as his personal envoys. Pope Benedict XVI beautifully summarized this when he stepped onto the balcony of St. Peter's for the first time. He said he was: "a simple and humble laborer in the vineyard of the Lord."[32] As the Bishop of Rome, he was in charge of everything in the Church, with full responsibility and power to bind and loose. He understood that this was to be done always as Jesus' representative, and that sooner or later he, as Josef Ratzinger, would become once again simply Josef, a humble servant of God. As the years of his post-papacy life unravel, his hiddenness and life of prayer have become a symbol of holiness for the whole Church.

Jesus gave us a parable about a vineyard. In the parable, the hired hands try to take over the vineyard itself, seeking to keep the fruits of

---

32 *Urbi et Orbi*, Apostolic Blessing of Pope Benedict XVI, April 19, 2005.

the vineyard for themselves. As long as they work simply and honorably, they have all they need and live life in peace. But as soon as they desire to conquer the vineyard for themselves, they become anxious, fearful, calculating, murderous, and evil. The vineyard becomes a dark place. Jesus used this image to decry some of the Jewish leadership of the time that were no longer shepherding the chosen people but instead acting as petty tyrants.

We are called to work with the Lord and closely hold his hand. As apostles of mercy, we do not have to fret over every detail; the solution to every problem does not depend solely on us. We participate in this mission as co-workers in the Lord's vineyard. It is his vineyard, not ours.

EASTER MONDAY

THE FRUSTRATED APOSTLES OF DIVINE MERCY

Right from the beginning of my ministry in St. Peter's See in Rome, I consider this message [of Divine Mercy] my special task. Providence has assigned it to me in the present situation of man, the Church and the world. It could be said that precisely this situation assigned that message to me as my task before God.
ST. JOHN PAUL II, NOVEMBER 22, 1981

Readings from the **Diary:** *718, 1747*

To be an apostle of Jesus means to ultimately desire to follow Jesus wherever he leads, and to work for his Kingdom the way Jesus wants. It is embracing whatever may come and striving to love as much as possible each day.

Jesus made very clear to Faustina that she was to be the secretary of Divine Mercy, to write down all he said and all she experienced. This writing was to be the basis of what Fr. Sopocko was to use to establish the Feast of Divine Mercy. Faustina was to bring him the writings, speak of her revelations, and support him by prayer. At the same time, Faustina was told by Jesus to leave her religious congregation and found a new one. In fact, Jesus even showed Faustina a vision of this new foundation, including the convent itself. These three tasks—establishing the Feast of Divine Mercy, painting the image, and founding the new congregation—were lifelong crosses for Faustina. All her life she tried as hard as she could to accomplish them, but at every step of the way, she was prevented from doing so. In fact, she complained to Jesus because she realized that it was at times Jesus himself who prevented her from accomplishing his will. Slowly Faustina realized that what was most important was trying to do God's will.

Faustina died before she completely fulfilled these requests of Jesus. The image was painted, although she admitted it did not capture perfectly the vision of Jesus. The new congregation was not yet founded. The Feast of Divine Mercy was not established by the Church in her lifetime. A divine catch-22 was at work. She could not do what God was asking her to do because God's plan was that she become a saint by simply "trying" to do his will as opposed to accomplishing his will. Thus, only in God's mind, and unaware to Faustina until the end of her life, she was accomplishing his will.

Fr. Sopocko had his own share of difficulties. He was told to establish the Feast of Divine Mercy and to spread the devotion far and wide. While he worked on this for many years, in his lifetime he never saw the feast day established. In fact, his somewhat brilliant ecclesial career was de-railed by this new assignment. He had to accept the humility of being an advocate for a visionary nun and writing about a topic that was not understood. This alienated him at times and made him somewhat of an oddity among his peers. Fr. Sopocko died without ever seeing the Feast of Divine Mercy accomplished.

The two apostles of Divine Mercy, Sr. Faustina and Fr. Sopocko, never accomplished in their lives the mission they felt God had called them to do. Yet, after the sacrifice of their lives, imitating the sacrifice of Christ, all they aspired to do was ultimately accomplished. The secret to their "divine success" is found in a simple but most essential teaching of Divine Mercy: that God rewards us also for our suffering, not only for our successes.

Jesus was faithful to his Father and died on the Cross. In human terms, Jesus was a failed Messiah on Good Friday. But in God's eyes, this dying in love brought redemption and grace into the world and was the secret to God's new plan.

A Christian who embraces Divine Mercy needs to undertake every project, every plan, and every prayer with this in mind. We are called to be faithful workers in the Lord's vineyard, and it is OK to not be a protagonist in the story. It is OK to work hard but see little fruits. It is OK that we struggle at times in our local Church milieu to have success. If I am daily looking to the heart of Christ and striving to love God by loving those around me, I am sure to accomplish his will. To live a life of Christian love is a transformative process that causes our hearts to be each day more like his.

Striving for success and accomplishment will always be a daily temptation. It is part of our human DNA. Yet our divine DNA will direct us toward fidelity and love. The divine reason behind this is that God's plans, which are mysterious to us, are always the most successful and awesome plans. Joining in his plan and faithfully following it is the path to the greatest success ever: union with God for all eternity.

EASTER TUESDAY

SPIRITUAL GENTLENESS

The steadfast love of the Lord never ceases, his mercies never come to an end.
LAMENTATIONS 3:22

Readings from the **Diary**: *299, 811, 848*

One of the greatest gifts of the diary of St. Faustina to the Church is that, reading through its pages, one is able to witness as a spectator the interaction of Jesus with a soul. This interaction, the way Jesus thinks and feels and speaks, gives us a glimpse into the heart of Jesus. It reveals the heights of holiness to which a soul can aspire and the incredible love that can exist in the world. This is the secret of Christianity: its driving force is always that of Divine Love! This Easter season, the loving exchanges between Faustina and Jesus will be crystallized in the light of spiritual gentleness.

The Gospels paint for us a picture of an incredible man, Jesus, who at once is on fire for truth and justice and at the same time delivers this truth and justice in the form of love. He conquers by his love. The Church uses a passage from the book of Wisdom in her Christmas liturgy:

> *For while all things were in quiet silence, and the night*
> *was in the midst of her course,*

Thy almighty word leapt down from heaven from thy royal throne, as a fierce conqueror into the midst of the land of destruction. (Wisdom 18:14–15)

This entrance of the divine into our world, the infinite entering the finite, the King of the Universe stepping into a fraction of his Kingdom, should have been, at least in the human mind, an explosive, extravagant event, remembered and recorded for all time. Yet this entrance was in hiddenness and peace. Jesus came not to destroy, but to woo. The closing episode of his life was on the Cross. He destroyed sin and death by allowing us to destroy him. He did not fight back but instead offered himself because of love. In the crucifixion of Our Lord is found the greatest symbol of Divine Love. Usually when we look at the crucifix, we see Our Lord suffering and think of our own sins that put him there. This is a healthy reminder of our fallen nature and the gift of salvation.

However, alongside our thoughts about our sins, it was not the intention of Jesus to give us a reminder that we have failed. His intention was to give us a reminder that we are loved. If I look to the Cross and can only see my sins, I have allowed the devil to once again steal from me the true image of God. As in Genesis, God the Father must remain in my heart as Father. And Jesus on the Cross must remain on the Cross as Savior, but my loving Savior. If I can see the smile from the Cross, that is an immense grace! Seeing the smile from the Cross does not mean forgetting my sins, but honestly accepting them before God. A person can love more in their own life if they see this crucified smile, which in turn becomes a force of love for them. The Cross cannot bring us fear alone; that will never be strength enough to walk the paths of love along which Our Lord wishes to lead us.

The theme of spiritual gentleness is a constant throughout Faustina's writings. Jesus refers often to his mercy as: "my tender mercy" (*Diary*, 299, 811, 848). He told Faustina that the feast day of Divine Mercy was born from the depths of his tenderness (see *Diary*, 699).

The words *tenderness* and *tender* in the English translation are not the exact words used in the original Polish. The Polish word is *wnętrzności*, which follows the Hebrew meaning of mercy as something to do with the maternity. It could be no other way.

Erasmo Leiva-Merikakis says:

> *Having mercy at bottom means bestowing life. God is merciful by nature because he is the Creator by nature. . . . One word for mercy in Hebrew . . . literally means the "viscera" occupying the abdominal region and, specifically, the womb. More profoundly this expression is metaphorically referring to God as a mother who has compassion on her children and feels it in that part of her body because it is there that she conceived them, bore them and gave them birth. . . . as matricial, or "having to do with the matrix" . . . but it points effectively to the concrete reality of mercy that is like a mother's womb continually bestowing new life.*[33]

Thus, the original Polish could be somewhat loosely rendered as "my motherly mercy" or "my life-giving mercy." The Incarnation of Jesus in the world, the Passion, Death, and Resurrection, are all born of the tender heart of our Savior. It is the reason for all that exists. These statements are powerful in their clarity and gentle in their essence. Simply put, we are loved, no matter how much we protest, as Peter did to Our Lord in the boat: "Go away from me, Lord, for I am a sinful man!" (Luke 5:8).

We will always be loved. Jesus is willing to be on the Cross for us as long as it takes to convince us of this.

---

33 Erasmo Leiva-Merikakis, *Fire of Mercy, Heart of the Word*, 198.

EASTER WEDNESDAY

A THEOLOGY OF SPIRITUAL GENTLENESS

*Our Lord tells us that the Kingdom of God grows imperceptibly and
slowly, due to the Mercy of God, which mysteriously takes possession
of human minds and hearts, and overcomes corruption and evil
passion. The spiritual life begins to unfold imperceptibly.*
BL. MICHAEL SOPOCKO, 100

Readings from the **Diary***: 1710, 1711, 1805, 1806*

When we look into the heart of Jesus, we are able to describe what we
find as a "tender Mercy" and a "spiritual gentleness." Jesus came as a fire
of love, full of passion and enthusiasm. But this was a gentle approach
as opposed to a destructive and violent approach. By this we mean that
Jesus' presence brings life and gives life. It brings water to the desert
of our souls, food to the hunger of our hearts, light for our eyes, and
joy to our hearts. This life-giving reality of Jesus is to be a model for an
apostle of mercy.

All too often we may encounter people, even "church people" that
seem to bring discord, tension, and anxiety wherever they go. These
types of people are the antithesis of an apostle of mercy. Imitating the
gentleness of Christ, whose yoke is easy and whose burden is light (see
Matthew 11:30) is not a passing fancy for sensitive souls. This is how
the Church should be and must be. How can we, as disciples of Christ,

imitate his gentleness? This has deeper consequences than at first may appear. Let us walk through a theology of this virtue.

The Christian who converts and leaves behind an old sinful way of life finds himself working to acquire the good habits of virtue and leaving behind the seven capital sins. We conquer our pride by our humility, our gluttony with our temperance, our lust with our chastity. After a time, a person can arrive at a stable place where, although occasional falls still happen, for the most part they are now no longer under the control of sin. While the capital sins may be somewhat behind us, we can't so quickly put behind us the seven *spiritual* sins. These are the capital sins but in their spiritual form—i.e., spiritual pride, spiritual envy, spiritual gluttony, and so on. One of them is the opposite of spiritual gentleness: spiritual wrath.

Spiritual wrath is to be impatient with oneself and with God. It is to get angry with oneself when one makes a mistake or sins. It is anger mostly because sin makes us look bad and reveals we are falling short of perfection. But the perfection we are seeking is not motivated by pure love for God, but a lot of love for self. We want to avoid sins because of how sin makes us feel, and we forget to avoid sin because it wounds the heart of God. Spiritual gentleness accepts its own limitations and weaknesses, always placing them before God.

Spiritual wrath also makes us impatient with God. We feel we deserve his blessings and grace NOW. If we have sinned, we feel God should have helped us more. We also demand what we want and don't wish to have to wait for it, and we want to be perfect NOW. To "let go and let God," as the saying goes, is never easy for the spiritually wrathful. Overcoming spiritual wrath is often a lifelong work.

Thus, a soul that is spiritually gentle gives God all the time he needs. Whatever God's mysterious plan is, the gentle soul is content with it. Perfection is seen as a fruit of love, a completeness in one's own life, and a journey to undertake. A gentle soul acknowledges that life is a process of sanctification in time, so it takes time. Being patient with

God means allowing him to do as he wishes. A gentle soul is free and is not driven to force anything. Gentleness lets God have his way!

A fruit of spiritual gentleness is peace of heart. The soul no longer panics, nor does it live an anxious and fretful life. Her prayer is peaceful. She brings her needs before God but spends more time thanking God for his blessings than reminding God of her needs. She goes to pray just to be with Jesus, not to get something done or accomplished. St. Thérèse famously once said that she did not mind falling asleep in prayer. This was because she went to pray for the sake of God alone, not for herself. A prayer in which she may have levitated and been in ecstasy was the same as falling asleep; it did not matter. What mattered was her desire to go to prayer and to spend time with God.

EASTER THURSDAY

THE CHARISM OF DIVINE SNUGGLING

Sister Faustina's spiritual life was accompanied by many mystical
phenomena . . .: external and interior visions, including hearing
words externally and interiorly. She also had many charisms –
the gift of reading souls, the gift of prophecy, as well as the gift of
"snuggling" her head up to the Hearts of Jesus and Mary.
EWA K. CZACZKOWSKA[34]

Readings from the **Diary***: 622, 104, 138, 960 1074*

In the *Diary*, Jesus has a tender way of inviting Faustina and the whole
world into his Sacred Heart. On four occasions, with insistence, he
tells Faustina to "snuggle" close to his heart (see *Diary*, 104, 138, 960,
1074). The Polish verb is *tulić*, which can only be translated as the
English word *snuggle*, and means exactly that. It is an affectionate and
prolonged embrace between a parent and child or between lovers. The
verb *to snuggle* may not resonate with certain people, especially men,
who are attracted more to the mission of Christ than the person of
Christ (although his mission is itself his person). Yet it is the way Jesus
deals with souls who become childlike and walk the paths of perfection.
The spiritual life becomes simpler toward the heights. It becomes union.

---

34 *Faustina, the Mystic and Her Message*, 100.

Jesus makes this invitation to be close to his heart so that we may be strengthened by his powerful divine love. A gentle soul that accepts this invitation may see a difficulty ahead on their path of life, but they go forward, confident that love conquers all. Nothing is too much to ask for love. No mountain too high to climb, no desert too long to traverse. A gentle soul has no hidden agenda, and hence is always the same person inside and out. They have no false masks behind which they operate.

A gentle soul keeps the truth of their life always before them. Such a soul has no need to always be the protagonist, but simply wishes to cooperate with God. Because she knows she can learn something from everyone, she is comfortable with everyone. Everyone is treated as a peer and as an equal. She never has to put on the false mask of control or superiority. These souls do not take themselves out of the category of "sinner." They know they need Jesus to save them each and every day, and therefore they accompany wayward souls alongside of them rather than ahead of them. As they go about their day, a gentle soul has a plan, but it is a "loose" plan. They make sure to be attentive and open to encounter whoever the Lord puts in their path. A spiritually gentle soul meets people where they are, and like St. Paul, becomes all things to all people (see 1 Corinthians 9:22).

When a soul like this gives spiritual advice, it is always adapted to the person they are advising, meeting them where they are and answering the questions they have in their heart. This is what God does. He runs out to meet the sinner. God's presence satisfies our deepest desires because he knows our deepest desires.

When Faustina was anxious or afraid, it was snuggling close to the heart of Christ that healed her. Ewa Czaczkowaska, in her biography of Faustina, calls this a *divine charism* of Faustina. In Faustina's life, snuggling close to the Sacred Heart of Jesus was the source of her strength. Divine snuggling is at its core allowing and permitting God to love us. It is taking down any barrier to his love in my life; it is laying down my weapons and allowing the Shepherd to gather me into his arms.

Lest any man who reads this feel that divine snuggling isn't something easy to understand, we have the example of St. John the Evangelist. John is a model for all men. He was comfortable with calling Jesus the Bridegroom and with calling himself the "Beloved Disciple." John understood and employed a "bridal theology" because first of all he was comfortable in his masculinity. For all who are able, men must at least understand the power and meaning behind this bridal theology. St. John the Evangelist bravely and confidently rested on the heart of Jesus at the Last Supper. Such a small thing, to rest for a moment on the heart of Jesus, yet that small thing became for John part of his claim to fame. As St. Thomas is the one who doubted, St. John is the one who rested. It may seem small, but John, like the theological eagle he was, in that moment was flying high in the paths of perfection, and he never came down.

EASTER FRIDAY

TOWARD A CHURCH OF MERCY

*"Holy Father, protect them in your name that you have
given me, so that they may be one, as we are one."*
JOHN 17:11

Readings from the **Diary:** *118, 651 1767*

All Christians are part of the mystical body of Christ, the Church.
Christians do not live in isolation. We are walking together, arm in
arm, on a pilgrim journey of faith toward our heavenly homeland. This
togetherness is a desire of Christ, as we see in the opening verse above.

Taken as a whole, the Church that Christ instituted on the rock
of St. Peter and that was born on Pentecost through the coming of
the Holy Spirit, is a Church whose mission is to be love in the world.
The Church will be a Church of mercy, or she will fail in her mission.
There is no better explanation of the Church of mercy than the vision
of Pope Francis laid out in his first major writing as Holy Father. In
Evangelii Gaudium ("The Joy of the Gospel"), he lays out a road map
for the Church.

One part of this road map is that the Church must *trust in God*.
Accepting mercy in our lives is not easy, and for the Church, trusting
in God more than in herself is likewise no easy task.

In a beautiful passage in the Gospels, Jesus instructs the apostles to not make provisions for the future, to not take extra money or sandals with them on the journey (see Matthew 10:10). He wants them to be a pilgrim people, on the move with nowhere to lay their heads. This itinerant style of life does not exclude the Church making long-lasting foundations, but it does mean the Church should always consider herself a pilgrim. If we try to make the Church focused on success in the world, we fall into spiritual worldliness. Pope Francis dedicates a few paragraphs to this evil to avoid.

> *Evangelization is the task of the Church. The Church,*
> *as the agent of evangelization, is more than an organic*
> *and hierarchical institution; she is first and foremost*
> *a people advancing on its pilgrim way towards God.*
> *She is certainly a mystery rooted in the Trinity, yet she*
> *exists concretely in history as a people of pilgrims and*
> *evangelizers, transcending any institutional expression,*
> *however necessary.*[35]

This type of "risky" Church, out in the street, bruised and dirty, demands a lot of faith. It is hard because it means the Church can never sit back and get comfortable but must always be on the lookout and ready to throw things aside.

The Lord's Church should be a trusting Church, not a worried Church, anxious Church, or protagonist Church. She is able to walk forward with gentleness and confidence because she is not trying to be the protagonist of everything. She knows how to accompany each one personally. Her message is always new and always going to the essentials of life as opposed to the arcane peripheries of thought.

Jesus gave us a powerful parable in the prodigal son (see Luke 15:11–32). The father in this parable lives in the world and embraces

---

35 *Evangelii Gaudium*, 111.

the world. He is out in the streets looking for his son. He does not preoccupy himself with the goings on of his house alone; he is in a sense at the door, not willing to shut the door and lock it until all his children have come home. He waits and is patient. As God takes his time with souls, the Church as well must take her time and keep the doors open. The Church exists to be a home for all, an ark of salvation in the world. For this reason, the Church will need be like the Father: full of mercy.

EASTER SATURDAY

THE QUEEN OF MERCY

She gave birth to her firstborn, and wrapped him in swaddling clothes and laid him in a manger.
LUKE 2:7

Readings from the **Diary***: 608, 625, 635, 785, 798, 844, 846*

Mary has a privileged and central role in the life of the Church. Mary's Immaculate Conception was perhaps the first gift of mercy. To allow God to enter and have free reign to work in our lives as he wishes is an attitude of deep trust. Mary let mercy become the essential reality of her life. She whispered, "Fiat," to the Angel Gabriel, which means "Let it be done!" (Luke 1:38). We must whisper our own Fiat to Divine Mercy, to accept and trust in this divine grace in our lives.

Mary appears about twenty times in the diary of Faustina. She accompanied Faustina throughout her religious life, interceding for her and encouraging her. Mary often appeared to Faustina around Christmas. During the Advent and Christmas season of 1936, Faustina dedicates a lot of time to writing in her diary (Notebook II). Faustina had become ill and was in a treatment center in Pradnik. During this time she was free from working long hours each day in the kitchen and garden, and thankfully she spent much time in prayer and journaling.

Mary appears to Faustina at the beginning of Advent and helps Faustina to get herself ready for Christmas.

Faustina notes that Mary appeared in this moment without the Child Jesus (*Diary*, 785). The secret to Advent according to the Blessed Mother is to live in deep silence, simple humility, and to let Jesus rest in your heart. Faustina is to live each day focused inward, aware of the presence of Christ in her soul. Mary is describing in a beautiful way how she must have lived her divine pregnancy. Those nine months would have been a time for Mary to converse with Jesus in her womb, to be focused on him and always aware of his presence.

Faustina dutifully puts these words of Mary into practice, helped by her seclusion in Pradnik. Faustina relished for once the ability to live as a Carmelite (*Diary*, 798), free from the work and study and prayers of her more Jesuit-styled congregation, and enjoy the quiet and hermit-like lifestyle of the Carmelites. This is a fruitful period of time for her.

As a gift, her religious community brought her home during the Christmas season so she would not have to spend Christmas alone. A Sr. Cajetan came to pick her up and bring her back to their convent. This trip through Cracow was well remembered by Faustina (*Diary*, 844). As they journeyed through Cracow, Faustina saw the people scurrying about in final preparations for Christmas Eve. Her monthlong stay at the treatment center had allowed her to experience silence and recollection and the presence of Christ. But seeing all the noise and hustle and bustle of the city, Faustina realized that most people are unable to truly prepare for Christmas as they ought. As they drove through the city, Faustina imagined Cracow to be another Bethlehem, where the people are not welcoming the baby Jesus into their homes.

A Christian who embraces Divine Mercy lives life aware of the presence of Christ in their soul. Their preparations for each feast day and each Christmas and Easter are both interior and exterior: exterior in the amount of love and service to their fellow man and interior in the amount of longing and desire that grow with each reception of the

Eucharist. Faustina longed to be able to tell the world about the great love in her heart, a love that all people can have if they only stop for a moment and look into their heart and their deepest longings.

The St. Faustina Blessing

When Faustina arrived home, she went to Midnight Mass at the convent. In that moment, one of the most special graces of Faustina occurred: Mary appeared to her, holding the Infant Jesus. She stepped close to Faustina and said: "My daughter, Faustina, take this most precious Treasure" (*Diary*, 846).

Mary calls Jesus her precious treasure. She is willing to share this treasure with Faustina often, mostly during the Christmas season. After Mary gives the infant Jesus to Faustina, she tends to step aside and leave Faustina and Jesus alone together (*Diary*, 608).

For Mary to freely give Jesus to Faustina and the world and then disappear into the background shows us a perfect example of what it means to be an apostle of mercy: to share the experience of Christ, to share our relationship with Christ, and then to step back and let Christ take over.

Each saint in the Church has a particular grace and blessing. It is possible to approach these saints in prayer and ask them to intercede for us and grant that same blessing. For Faustina, her blessing is to receive from Mary the child Jesus, who appears to us in simplicity to teach us simplicity. Asking Faustina for this grace is a beautiful way to grow as an apostle of Divine Mercy. We bring Jesus with us, the simple and loving Jesus of mercy, and present this treasure to souls. We don't present ourselves; we don't try to be the protagonist; we are just channels for Christ to work.

This also is the image of the Church and how the Church must be "Marian" at her core. This is to be an instrument of mercy, to allow Jesus to live and dwell and work through us by giving our own personal *Fiat* to God.

DIVINE MERCY SUNDAY

***

WALKING BY MERCY'S LIGHT

*Mercy overcomes every wall, every barrier, and leads you to always
seek the face of the man, of the person. And it is mercy which
changes the heart and the life, which can regenerate a person and
allow him or her to integrate into society in a new way.*
POPE FRANCIS, SEPTEMBER 14, 2014

Readings from the **Diary***: 49, 474, 475, 570, 949, 1075, 1572*

We now arrive at the Feast of Mercy! We have many hidden apostles of
Divine Mercy to thank for this feast day. As well, there were many men
and women of the Church who worked hard to make this feast day a
reality. They each allowed themselves to walk *by Mercy's light*.

For starters, there is St. Faustina. After coming to the end of these
reflections, the story that is revealed is of a woman who suffered much
for God. She had to forsake her beloved family at a young age. This
small sacrifice, a life lived far from home, may get lost amid the bigger
happenings of Divine Mercy. Yet Faustina took on this personal sacrifice
with love. As well, we remember how she boarded a train with almost
nothing, going to a city she had never lived in, and risked everything
for Jesus. We need today to thank her for those many sacrifices that
made the story of Divine Mercy possible.

We also have Bl. Michael Sopocko. This brilliant priest sacrificed much on a personal level to take up the burden of Divine Mercy. Being associated with Divine Mercy did not initially bring him much public honor and recognition. Yet he kept going, step-by-humble step, with the work of mercy.

St. John Paul II was an essential part of this story. His pontificate was long and storied. He had humble beginnings in Poland and was an orphan who suffered much during the war. Yet he is known today as a saint, a mystic, and a scholar who pointed the whole world to Christ. He was the pope who made today's feast a reality.

Today we are joined by the saints and angels in heaven, who are all gathered around the throne of the Lamb to glorify Divine Mercy. Today we should commit to keeping these elements of devotion to Divine Mercy in our minds and hearts:

- *the image of the Merciful Jesus (Diary, 49)*
- *the Feast of the Divine Mercy on the Second Sunday of Easter (Diary, 49)*
- *the Chaplet of Divine Mercy (Diary, 474–476)*
- *the hour of Mercy (Diary, 1572)*
- *spreading the honor of Divine Mercy (Diary, 1075)*

As Christians in the world today, we must remember to focus on the Corporal and Spiritual Works of Mercy. To evangelize and spread the Good News, we need witnesses, not ideas. We need saints, not activists. To live as an apostle of Divine Mercy is to make the following activities a real part of one's life.

Corporal Works of Mercy
Give drink to the thirsty
Shelter the homeless
Visit the sick
Visit the prisoners

Bury the dead
Visit the cemetery and pray for those you have lost.
Give alms to the poor

Spiritual Works of Mercy
Counsel the doubtful
Instruct the ignorant
Admonish the sinner
Comfort the sorrowful
Forgive injuries
Bear wrongs patiently
Pray for the living and the dead

Throughout this Lent, we have been seeking to walk *by Mercy's Light*. Some of the great themes in this book have been chosen to help one to slowly become an apostle of Divine Mercy. We are invited to accept the loving invitation of Jesus to begin the dance of mercy in our own life. We learn that a love-centered approach to the spiritual life will aid us in accomplishing the important work of accepting Divine Mercy. We are invited to walk with Jesus as Faustina did, in trust and childlike simplicity, shouldering the cross with Jesus, seeking to in some small way to console his Sacred Heart. A milestone in our spiritual life will be reached when we allow a spiritual gentleness to permeate our soul. A fruit of Divine Mercy in our life will be that we become apostles of a mercy in the world, and thus keep alive the final words of Jesus to his apostles and disciples:

> *"Go therefore and make disciples of all nations, baptizing them in the name of the Father and of the Son and of the Holy Spirit, teaching them to observe all that I have commanded you; and lo, I am with you always, to the close of the age."* (Matthew 28:19–20)

Today, as you pray the Chaplet, I invite you to end with the litany of praise to Divine Mercy found in the *Diary* (949). To close, pray with St. John Paul II the following prayer he gave in 2002 while in Poland at the Shrine of Divine Mercy:

God, merciful Father,
in your Son, Jesus Christ, you have revealed your love
and poured it out upon us in the Holy Spirit, the
    Comforter,
We entrust to you today the destiny of the world
and of every man and woman.

Bend down to us sinners,
heal our weakness,
conquer all evil,
and grant that all the peoples of the earth
may experience your mercy.
In You, the Triune God,
may they ever find the source of hope.

Eternal Father,
by the Passion and Resurrection of your Son,
have mercy on us and upon the whole world!
Amen.

For information on bulk pricing for parishes and
book-study groups, contact the author at:
bymercyslight@gmail.com

Made in the USA
Monee, IL
29 January 2022